Plato's Parmenides

Albert Keith Whitaker

Junior Olin Fellow
University of Chicago

Focus Philosophical Library
Focus Publishing/R. Pullins Company
PO Box 369
Newburyport MA 01950

The Focus Philosophical Library

Plato's Sophist • E. Brann, P. Kalkavage, E. Salem • 1996
Plato's Parmenides • Albert Keith Whitaker • 1996
Plato's Symposium • Avi Sharon • 1998
Plato's Phaedo • E. Brann, P. Kalkavage, E. Salem • 1998
Plato's Republic • Joe Sachs • 2007
Empire and the Ends of Politics • S. D. Collins and D. Stauffer • 1999
Four Island Utopias • D Clay, A. Purvis • 1999
Plato's Timaeus • P. Kalkavage • 2001
Aristotle's Nicomachean Ethics • Joe Sachs • 2002
Hegel's The Philosophy of Right • Alan White • 2002
Socrates and Alcibiades: Four Texts • David M. Johnson • 2003
Plato's Phaedrus • Stephen Scully • 2003
Plato's Meno • George Anastaplo and Laurence Berns • 2004
Spinoza's Theologico-Political Treatise • Martin Yaffe • 2004
Plato's Theaetetus • Joe Sachs • 2004
Aristotle: Poetics • Joe Sachs • 2005

ISBN 10: 0-941051-96-X
ISBN 13: 978-0-941051-96-5

10 9 8 7 6 5 4 3 2

1006TS

Contents

To Paul White

The main event in the arising of philosophy is the discovery of the asking of this question, the unasked question about the One. Wherever in its history instead of repeating its birth it does something else, philosophy is merely the name of a name.

Kurt Riezler, Parmenides

Introduction

The most pressing fact that faces the student of Plato's *Parmenides* is the replacement of Socrates by Parmenides. In most Platonic dialogues we meet an old yet sprightly Socrates who eagerly discusses matters of great moral importance with young men, often more handsome than intelligent. But for most of this dialogue Parmenides takes the role of mature interlocutor, first with a very young Socrates himself, and then with another young man named Aristotle. Who is Parmenides? Who is this young Socrates? And what are they talking about? The subject is certainly not the usual Socratic fare: the just, the beautiful, the good. Instead we face a long, complicated and seemingly scientific discussion of the most abstract matters: Forms, the One, the Many. When beginning the *Parmenides* it is helpful to keep the last lines in mind:

> So it looks, whether one *is* or *is* not, both it and the different things, both in relation to themselves and in relation to each other, all, in all ways, both *are* and *are* not and both appear and do not appear.
>
> Most true.[1]

These lines, as does all that precedes them, force the reader to ask without fail, "What is going on here?"

A Beginning

Who was Plato? The man was born and died in the Greek city of Athens; he lived from 427 B.C. to 347 B.C. According to the ancient canon his life's

---

[1] Wherever in the introduction or in the translation the verb "to be" or one of its many forms is italicized, the verb should be taken in the existential rather than copulative sense. The reason the verb "to exist" is not used instead is that "exist" has a locative and assertive sense that "to be" does not. One could say that it is Parmenides' very point, in this dialogue, to force us to give up thinking about the highest things, such as Being, in such imagistic terms.

work is a corpus of thirty-six dialogues (his letters the old scholars counted as one "dialogue"), which after his death was divided into nine tetralogies (groups of four). The *Parmenides* is the first dialogue of the third tetralogy, whose other members are the *Philebus, Symposium* and *Phaedrus*. In modern times scholars have labored greatly to try to determine Plato's "development" as a thinker and writer; they have thus directed their main efforts towards establishing an order to Plato's writings. This attempt, though whole-hearted and prosecuted with great skill, has left us only with stale results and controversy. Not the least problem for this approach is the ancient report that Plato wrote and rewrote his dialogues continuously throughout his long life. Since confusion hobbles the "developmental" approach, and as this is a volume for newcomers to the *Parmenides*, I have thought it best, while allowing us to follow up any dramatic hints towards other dialogues, simply to try to learn what the *Parmenides* on its own can teach us.

And that, in itself, is no light task. The *Parmenides* is, to put it mildly, a puzzle. No other Platonic dialogue leaves its reader with such a sense of *aporia* or "being without anywhere to go." If you stick with it, and read it carefully, you will end with many more questions than when you began. So why read the thing, if it is so tedious and, ultimately, so unsatisfying? I hope this introduction may provide some incentive and some guidance. But before you conclude that the profundity of the *Parmenides* is too serious, too weighty, too imposing for you even to attempt to plumb it, recall the story of the wise professor who, one hour of leisure while he was laughing and playing with some friends, spied a pretentious colleague drawing near. "My boys," he said, "let us be grave: here comes a fool." The *Parmenides* will respond best to your wonder if you not only approach it willing to work, but with a sense of humor as well.

But why should we try to understand this puzzling work? A possible answer is that we wish to understand better the life and thought of the greatest philosopher in history, Socrates. Besides the works of Plato, there are two other accounts of Socrates' life by people who knew him, the *Clouds* of the comic poet Aristophanes and the Socratic dialogues of the philosopher Xenophon. If we imagine all these sources as giving us moments in the life of Socrates, a sort of scattered biography of the man, then we will soon recognize that the *Parmenides* offers us the first dramatic picture of Socrates' life; that is, the *Parmenides* presents Socrates as younger than we ever see him elsewhere. Furthermore, the *Parmenides* is the only example we possess of a conversation between Socrates, albeit a very young Socrates, and another philosopher. By studying this dialogue, then, we may learn something about the source of Socratic philosophy, especially as it relates to earlier Greek philosophy.

But the question of the genesis of Socratic philosophy is, one may contend, a historical question. Is there anything timeless in this dialogue for us to learn? Anything that should interest us not as historians of ancient greek philosophy, but as human beings? Most basically, this dialogue concerns the Forms and the One. To put it loosely, the Forms are the principles or the sources of explanation of all the parts of the whole: earth, fire, dog, man, even moral qualities such as justice and prudence. When Socrates asks, "What is…?" about something, he begins a quest to know the form of that thing. On the other hand, the One is the principle or the source of our knowledge of the Whole itself. We human beings recognize that we live in a World. This World, as a "this," is One. In other words, to combine our various and changing perceptions with knowledge of the Forms and knowledge of the One would be to know the whole of things entirely, from top to bottom, as one whole together with the many parts.

Such a dream of comprehensivity would, I think, sound strange (and yet attractive) to any listener of any time. But it sounds especially strange to us, as we are taught from our earliest youth to eschew such comprehensivity in favor of the abstractness of modern science. Some simple examples may make clearer what I mean. When a surgeon operates on a hand, he has in mind the hand he learned about in anatomy class, a static collection of bones, muscles, veins and arteries, an unmoving and lifeless thing. Thankfully for the patient, his understanding of his own hands is quite different. He knows his own hands as parts of a whole, as entities that feel pain and enjoy pleasure, that move with suppleness and grace, that can follow directions towards what he thinks is good but which cannot do everything he would like. The hand in his mind and those at the ends of his arms share little in common, and yet he calls them all "hand." An example even closer to home for philosopy students is that of a thinker and his thought. You may learn in psychobiology that thought is the action and interaction of electrical impulses, drawn along neurons in our brains by the combination of myriad chemicals. You may think about these wondrous happenings. And yet does electricity and chemicals explain your wonder? Do they explain why you think self-examination is good? Indeed, all of our thoughts and actions aim at some good. But what can bones, muscles, chemicals or electricity tell us about the good? They fall mute. Even our thought, our very selves, we divide in two: the thought we think and the thought we think about.

My contention is not that the surgeon's anatomical image of the hand and the biochemist's description of thought are simply wrong. But they are incomplete. They leave out or ignore significant aspects of our living experience of these phenomena. Our understanding of the hand wants to be one. We do not want to be of two minds about thought. The union of the One and the Many is not simply an ancient Greek concern. It is a passion that human beings of every age can feel, the passion to know the whole. The exciting thing about this dialogue, the *Parmenides*, is that it directly addresses this concern and this passion. And it does so by speaking to a young, inexperienced, and promising fellow who has many of the same wonders that we do.

Outline

The *Parmenides* falls into three major parts: the introduction or proemium (126a1-127a7), the conversations between Socrates and Zeno and then Socrates and Parmenides (127a8-137c3), and the long dialogue between Aristotle and Parmenides (137c4-166c5).[2]

Narration: The *Parmenides* is a narrated dialogue, meaning that we, the readers, "hear" about the events of the dialogue from someone; we do not "see" the dialogue happening as though it were on stage. In this case the narrator is a largely unknown fellow named Cephalus who heard the dialogue from a certain Antiphon, who in turn learned the conversation by heart from Pythodorus, who did witness it in person, decades before. The *Parmenides* shares this very strange, thrice-removed style of narration with only one other Platonic dialogue, the *Symposium*, whose subject is *eros* or passionate love.

Introduction (126a1-127a7): Cephalus speaks of how he once visited Athens and learned the details of an old conversation between Socrates, Zeno and Parmenides from Antiphon, the half-brother of Glaucon and Adeimantus, who are themselves the brothers of Plato. Antiphon was once an eager student of philosophy, which is why he memorized this entire piece. But this great labor was not effective in engendering a philosophic life. Now he spends his time on horses.

Socrates and Zeno (127a8-130a2): The scene is Athens at the very center of the fifth century. Zeno and Parmenides, two of the greatest philosophers of the time, have come to the city in the midst of a grand civic festival so that Zeno could read his famous "speeches" about the Many. Young Socrates confronts the mature Zeno (who is said to be Parmenides' lover) about Zeno's demonstration that what *is* cannot be many. We note the strangeness, perhaps even the silliness of Zeno's claim. Socrates earnestly puts forward his own claim, that what truly *is* are a number of "forms," in which everything else partakes and from which everything receives its name. Socrates stipulates that these forms, once posited, explain away our wonder at or confusion over the

---

[2] All references to Platonic texts in the introduction and in the footnotes to the translation will be to the edition of Stephanus. Stephanus, Henri Estriénne was his proper name, was an outstanding German printer and scholar who lived from 1528-1598. The page and paragraph divisions of his 1578 edition of Plato are retained in all modern editions. Since the lines of this translation do not accord exactly with the lines of Stephanus, the student should disregard the last number given in any citations. For example, read "127a7" as late in paragraph 127a.

things we see and talk about.

Socrates and Parmenides (130a3-137c3): Parmenides praises Socrates for his zeal but levels devastating criticisms of his forms. First Parmenides shows the impossibility of explaining how the things among us "participate" in these forms. Then he argues that if these forms exist, each on its own, it is impossible for us to know anything about them. But, in close, he admits that if we do not posit a form for each thing, our minds will have nothing firm to fasten upon and communication will be impossible. In the face of this paradox, Parmenides proposes that Socrates train in a sort of "gymnastic" before he tries again to posit individual forms on their own.

Aristotle and Parmenides (137c4-166e5): Parmenides then illustrates, with Aristotle, what he means by his gymnastic: it consists in making hypotheses and deducing the results. Parmenides takes, as the subject of his hypothesizing, the One, which he calls his own hypothesis. He first hypothesizes that the One *is*, and twice shows the results for the One itself and twice for the things different than the One. Then he hypothesizes that this same thing, the One, *is* not, and twice shows the results for the One and twice again for the different things. What are the results?

Argument One: if One *is*, the One experiences nothing (137c4-142a7). *Argument Two*: if the One *is*, the One experiences all things (142a8-155e3). He then "speaks again for a third time," and argues that when the One *is* in "the instant," it *is* nothing, but otherwise it can experience all things (155e4-157b5). *Argument Three*: if the One *is*, the things different than it experience all things (157b6-159b1). *Argument Four*: if the One *is*, the different things suffer nothing at all (159b2-160b1). (He then makes a brief summation of his results.) *Argument Five*: if the One *is* not, it must suffer all sorts of things (160b5-163b6). *Argument Six*: if the One *is* not, it can suffer nothing (163b7-164b4). *Argument Seven*: if the One *is* not, the different things appear to suffer all sorts of things (164b5-165e1). *Argument Eight*: if the One *is* not, then the different things do not and do not appear to suffer anything (165e2-166c2). Once more, he briefly summarizes what has come before.

Parmenides

We know very little about Parmenides' life. His home was Elea, a town in south-western Italy which was founded around 535 B.C. by Phocaea, a Greek city on the coast of Asia Minor. Parmenides was said to be a student of the philosopher Xenophanes, a man who roamed about Greece criticizing Homer and Hesiod for their all-too-human portrayals of the Gods and who seemed to advocate monotheism. As we learn from this dialogue, one of Parmenides' own pupils was Zeno, and he also decisively influenced the Samian philosopher Melissus.[3]

Parmenides, it is said, produced only one written work, a poem in heroic verse of which we now possess but fragments. The poem falls into three major parts: the introduction or proemium, the "Way of Truth," and the "Way of Opinion." In the proemium Parmenides himself narrates to us how he was conveyed, by a horse-drawn chariot, to the "Gate of Night and Day," which was opened for him by the goddess Justice. Once past the gate he met another, unnamed goddess who took his hand and told him the rest of the poem, which covers "the unwavering heart of well-rounded truth" as well as "the opinions of mortal men, in which there is no true trust." In the largely-preserved "Way of Truth," the goddess tells us about Being, which she insists *is* and cannot ever have come into being or cease to be. In fact, she warns us repeatedly to keep our minds and our speech away from claiming that Being *is* not or that what *is* not, *is*. To claim that Being *is* not or that Non-being *is*, is a road that is "unthinkable and unnamable," she says. The "Way of Opinion," in contrast, though deceitful and untrustworthy, is the road that most mortals travel upon, mixing together what *is* and what *is* not and becoming lost in appearances. The goddess offers to tell us about this way so that we may not be deceived as well. This third part of the poem seems to consist of a familiar sort of physical description of the cosmos, of the order of the Sun, Moon, stars and elements. All three parts of the poem are enigmatic and mysterious. They seem purposely designed by Parmenides to keep his truth "far from the wanderings of men."

Why, then, is this eccentric Eleatic the subject of Plato's dialogue? Why don't we have a *Heraclitus* or a *Democritus* instead? Socrates gives us a hint why Parmenides, in particular, may be worthy of honor. In a conversation at the end of his life, Socrates said that Parmenides alone, of all previous thinkers and writers, did not belong to "the army" of Homer.[4] It was the conviction of this army, he says, that "no one thing, in itself, *is*" and that "nothing ever *is*, but always becomes." Socrates cites as an example of this belief in (near) universal flux and becoming, Homer's line, "Ocean and Mother Tethys, the genesis of the Gods" (*Iliad* 14.302). Though like the other early thinkers Parmenides veiled his thought with poetry, in contrast, claims Socrates, Parmenides did *not* believe that flux and perception reign supreme. "Being *is*," is the divine word of Parmenides, which echoes down, through the aeons,

---

[3] Based on this very dialogue, whose dramatic date is around 450 B.C., scholars determine that Parmenides was born about 515 B.C. (see 127b3 and 127c5). However, another ancient tradition held that Parmenides flourished in 500 B.C., meaning that he was born in 540 B.C. If this tradition is correct, then a meeting between the young Socrates and Parmenides would have been impossible and would have to be considered an invention of the poetic Plato.

[4] *Theaetetus* 152d-153a. A good English translation of this text is that of Seth Benardete, *Plato's Theaetetus*, University of Chicago, 1984, pp. 15-16.

even to our day. Change does not change; motion does not move; becoming does not come to be. Being *is*, and hence knowledge and truth may *be*. For Parmenides, "well-rounded truth" or wisdom is a possibility, whether or not it takes a great deal of searching or even divine intercession to find. In other words, Socrates teaches us that, in his eyes at least, Parmenides is the true founder of philosophy, the love of and search for wisdom.

But the Parmenides we meet in the poem does not appear to be the Parmenides we meet in Plato's dialogue. This Parmenides does not speak of mystical journeys in dactylic verse; if anything, his arguments with Aristotle have a mathematical, not a poetic, appearance. Those arguments also ostensibly concern the hypothesis of "the One," which at 137b1 Plato's Parmenides calls "my hypothesis." In his poem Parmenides speaks of Being, not One. Most surprisingly, in the fifth argument with Aristotle, at 162a-b, our Parmenides shows that, in a way, Non-being must *be*, a pronouncement we cannot imagine the goddess on the Way of Truth would allow. Plato, the creator of this dialogue and all that is said in it, is also a poet of sorts, even though he does not write in verse. What has spurred his poetic imagination to present such an incongruous Parmenides?

Not only do many of Parmenides' deductions in the dialogue contradict the words of his poem, they all, on the surface, contradict one another. But surely Plato did not put these seemingly ridiculous and contradictory speeches in Parmenides' mouth as a way to insult the ancient thinker. Leaving aside the praise of Parmenides which Plato puts into Socrates' mouth in the *Theaetetus*, if Plato meant this dialogue as a joke on Parmenides, surely it is the most tedious joke in all of literature! And Plato is adept at making jokes. We can reject, then, the hypothesis that the *Parmenides* is Plato's attempt at philosophical slander.

But we have noticed that Plato's Socrates, and hence Plato himself, knew that older thinkers like Parmenides and Homer used poetic devices to hide their teachings from the many. In this dialogue Parmenides does not speak poetically and he speaks before only a few people, not many, as is twice noted (see 136d7 and 136a7). So do we surmise, from these dramatic hints, that what Plato presents in this dialogue in Parmenides' mouth, is the unvarnished truth of the great old man's own poem, stripped of its poetic guise; the Way of Truth, so to speak, alone and without the misleading Way of Opinion?

This conjecture is attractive, but we must intrude several deep qualifications. First, Plato presents nothing "stripped" of poetry. The dialogue itself is a poetic creation, if anything even more puzzling than Parmenides' poetry since nowhere does the poet, Plato, address us in his own voice. Second, everything Parmenides says here is said for the benefit of young Socrates, a very young Socrates (see 136a-c and 126c). Why — how? — would an old and thoughtful philosopher such as Parmenides expound his knowledge to such a neophyte, albeit a promising one? Parmenides himself remarks that Socrates is not yet ready to see the truth; he needs training (136c). If everything that Plato's Parmenides says were the truth of Parmenides' poem, then, leaving aside the ubiquitous contradictions, we can say that the only result of Parmenides' exposition would be to engender belief in young Socrates, belief that these arguments present the truth, since the young man is not in the position to know the truth himself. He, and we, cannot rest content with belief in what others say; we must work for knowledge. Parmenides' speeches dramatically hammer home this lesson, for they all contradict one another. On the surface Parmenides' words appear both silly and solemn; but in their essence they can be neither empty, self-inflicted raillery nor unvarnished truth. As we learn from Parmenides' poem itself, the Way of Truth and the Way of Opinion or Appearance must not be separated; they come together in one whole. The poetic surface of these works is not an obstacle to be removed by the serious reader. Indeed, it is itself a reflection of and a way into their complex cores. If nothing else, that is one lesson that Plato learned from Parmenides.

Zeno

One of Parmenides' characteristics that Plato emphasizes in this dialogue is that he was, and may still be, a man of passion, a lover.[5] Perhaps, then, we may come to understand better the speech of Plato's Parmenides by considering his lover and student Zeno.

Though we know even less about Zeno than about his teacher, Zeno's fame is his paradoxes. One of these is about an arrow in flight. Zeno says that, because at every instant the arrow is in a space equal to itself, it must at every instant be at rest. Therefore the arrow, though it appears to move, is in fact motionless. One could also say that, because at every moment "now" we are the same age as ourselves, we in fact never get older; the flow of time is merely apparent. And yet we know by experience that the arrow does move and hit its target and that we do get older and die.

As we learn from this dialogue, Zeno also poses paradoxes about the One and the Many. In the dialogue he uses an argument, to which Socrates objects, to argue that what *is* must be one. That is, he denies that what truly *is* is many, right in the face of all our everyday experience. But arguments preserved outside of this dialogue show even more completely how Zeno clinches a paradox on this topic, forcing his listeners to reject mutually contradictory opinions. For example, when he wants to show that what *is* cannot be many

---

[5] At 127b we learn that Zeno was said to have been Parmenides' young beloved years before. But at 137a, right before embarking on the pseudo-mathematical arguments of the gymnastic, Parmenides quotes from a poem where the poet, also an old man, describes himself, at his age, falling in love.

he would point out that the Many must be as many as they *are* — no more nor less —, and thus be finite in number. But since they are many, truly many, there must always be things between them, and things between those things, and hence the things that *are* are infinite — a contradiction. So, then, one might say, what *is* is one. Not so fast. If what *is* is one, Zeno would say, it cannot have magnitude. If it did have magnitude, it would be divisible, infinitely so, and would thus become as many as its parts and perhaps even dissolve into nothing. So what *is*, which is one, has no magnitude. But whatever has no magnitude, if it be added to something it will make that something no larger, nor if it be subtracted will it make that something smaller. But what makes no change when added or subtracted *is* not; it is nothing at all. What *is* cannot be what is *not*. So what *is* cannot be many or one. And yet, logically, it must be.

Young Socrates was not the last person to attack Zeno for what he thought were specious arguments, resulting in merely apparent contradiction. The philosopher Aristotle, in his *Physics*, also criticizes Zeno for what he takes to be Zeno's tactic of using unwarranted assumptions to set an argument askew.[6] Now Zeno himself admits, in the dialogue, that he wrote arguments of this sort out of a love of victory or fighting (128c-e). Trickery and dodges may be par for the course in a fight. Let us not, then, incur blame for similarly improper moves by treating Zeno as he may have treated others.

What then does Zeno's way of speaking teach us? He was known, in antiquity, as "double-tongued." The epithet is fitting, for his arguments proceed by laying before us two alternatives; for example, rest and motion, the moment and the progress of time, unity and multiplicity. What he then does is to show us that each of the two alternatives, left to itself, raises a contradiction. The whole cannot be one, but it cannot be many. Our mind, then, is left in a paradox, something, literally, "against our opinion." One and many are mutually exclusive, just as are rest and motion, the moment and the movement of time. Each is impossible. Both, then, *together*, must be true. What we *call* motion we *know* as both rest and motion, a strange mixture of position and the change from here to there. What we *call* time we *know* as both timelessness and time, a strange mixture of the "now" and the progress from the "was" to the "will be." What we *call* the One or the Whole we *know* as both whole or one and as parts or many, a strange mixture of unsatisfying but accessible parts and a longed-for but mysterious wholeness or unity. Zeno's arguments, far from being verbal trickery or manipulation, bring out into the open the latent questions that our own ways of speaking carefully keep alive. At one moment we speak of time as discrete moments; at another we speak of

---

[6] See *Physics* 239b ff. for several paradoxes and Aristotle's critique. For a translation the reader may wish to consult *The Complete Works of Aristotle*, edited by Jonathan Barnes, Princeton University Press, 1984, volume one, pp. 404 ff.

it as indivisible flow. We want to abandon neither, for both, though they contradict one another, speak some truth about what we call time.

Zeno's speech forces the mind to hold-together and see as apparent two very attractive appearances. Each reveals itself to be "merely" apparent because neither one can explain away the other. Neither is acceptable alone, but they defy speech when the understanding holds them together. Based on these formulations we can begin to see the connection between the pupil and the teacher. Zeno's double-tongued arguments achieve the same result as Parmenides' poetic presentation of the Way of Truth. According to the Way of Truth, in a similar way to Zeno's arguments, our everyday opinion about the whole — that in it all sorts of things *are* not or are some weird mixture of Being and Non-being — is merely an opinion; it is mere appearance or partial. Being *is* and Non-being *is* not, just as the moving arrow is in fact at rest. But we know that the whole cannot simply be Being, as surely as it cannot simply be Non-being. Every moment we experience that what *is was* not, what will *be is* not yet. Thus the Way of Truth is followed by the Way of Opinion. Taken on its own the Way of Opinion is misleading. It unknowingly mixes together the two most different things, Being and Non-being, in the same way as everyday speech about time thoughtlessly mixes together progress and timelessness. But once we have been led to the Way of Truth by Parmenides, we can see that the Way of Opinion, misleading and thoughtless as it may be, in fact reflects unknowingly the paradoxical mixture that is the Whole. Parmenides poetically breaks apart the whole, implicitly challenging us with the impossibility of leaving the two alternatives, Being and Non-being, separate on their own, but as well with the feeling of paradox and speechlessness at trying to combine them as one.[7]

Before we noticed that the Parmenides of the poem speaks about Being while Plato's Parmenides speaks about the One, and we wondered at this difference. Now we can see the reason for the change. By making his Parmenides speak about the One rather than Being, Plato allows us to see the genius of Parmenides' thought, a genius which belongs as well to Zeno's speeches and all later philosophy that deserves the name. This genius is the passion, the erotic desire, to know the whole as one, not a simple and undifferentiated one, but as a one that remains complex and questionable to its very core.[8]

---

[7] Thus when, in argument five, Plato's Parmenides deduces that, in a way, Non-being *is*, he is in fact in harmony with Parmenides' poem, rightly understood.

[8] But why does Plato present Parmenides as spending most of his time talking with a certain young Aristotle? We noticed above how Aristotle the philosopher, Plato's own pupil, does not see Zeno's paradoxes as raising questions about the greatest things, such as motion, time and the whole, but rather as using verbal dodges to confuse listeners. We may add that, though in his *Metaphysics* Books A and M

Young Socrates and the Forms

Notwithstanding that Plato claims, in his *Second Letter*, that all the writings that are supposedly his truly belong to a "Socrates who's become young and beautiful" (314c), we see no more of Socrates' actual youth in the dialogues than the *Parmenides* itself. The *Parmenides*, as we have noted, is the first moment in Socrates' dialogic life. But in the *Phaedo*, the last episode of this life, Socrates himself tells us something about his youth. He tells us about his wonder, as a young man, at natural phenomena; about his dissatisfaction with previous scientists' explanations; about his turn to, and from, Anaxagoras; and, finally, about his "second sailing," when he "fled" from these physical investigations into speeches in order to learn the truth of the beings (96a-100b).[9] How does this turn from physics to speeches relate to what we see happening in the *Parmenides*?

As Parmenides himself mentions twice, young Socrates enjoys a great "zeal for speeches" at the time of this dialogue (130b1 and 135d3). Does this remark indicate that Socrates is not simply a student of physics at this point; has he already taken up the oars? In any event, we can conclude that the "gymnastic" that Parmenides offers is not meant to move physicists into dialectic. The gymnastic does not awaken a zeal for speeches, but depends upon its pre-existence.

Socrates also is quite attached to the notion of forms. Did he himself come up with this idea? That is Parmenides' first question of him (130b2-3). Socrates gets caught up with other concerns and does not answser Parmenides' question; the drama of the dialogue, however, does. Their conversation makes clear how the idea of forms could arise: from "looking" at things. As Parmenides conjectures, whenever Socrates looks at many great things, he recognizes, as he's looking, that all the particular great things share one and the same "look," The sameness and unity of this "look," in turn, make him imagine that there exists, somewhere, some Greatness in itself, separate from the many great

---

Aristotle attacks Socrates' "forms" with the very same arguments that Parmenides levels in this dialogue, the *Parmenides* is the only major Platonic dialogue not referred to by name in the Aristotelian corpus. This is not the place to begin an inquiry into the differences between Plato and Aristotle. Let me say simply that to begin such an inquiry one would do well to consider Aristotle's treatment of the greatest things with that of the *Parmenides*. Young Aristotle in this dialogue does not act at all concerned with the numerous paradoxes and questions that Parmenides' speech raises.

[9] The "second sailing" does not mean that Socrates started out anew a second time or was heading somewhere different. It is a nautical expression, referring to the moment the sailors turn to oars when the wind deserts their sails. One might render it as his "second-best" sailing. For the *Phaedo*, see the forthcoming translation by Brann et al. (Focus Philosophical Library).

things (132a1-4). The birth of the forms seems to lie in the eye of the beholder, thus the words "form" and "idea," in Greek, both derive from the verb "to see." Sight persuades us that the world is grouped into "classes" or "kinds." And yet it is speeches where the forms, and their power, truly come to light. Our visual intimation that there is some Greatness that makes all the many great things great is born out in our speeches to one another about the great things, where "great" means one thing and "small" another and "equal" yet a third. As Parmenides and Socrates both agree, if someone does not allow that there is always an idea, the same one, for each of the beings, he will entirely destroy the power of conversation. When all is flux, speech is chatter.

However, young Socrates' turn to forms has not made him a lover of wonder or a lover of speeches. In fact, he is eager to use his imagined forms to explain away the wonder of the visual world and to render speech scientific, exact and powerful. As he says to Zeno, there is no wonder in recognizing that things in the world partake of both likeness and unlikeness, unity and multiplicity (see 129a-e). To put it another way, why be amazed that your fourth finger is both small (in comparison to your middle finger) and large (in respect to your fifth finger) at the same time? By positing the forms, Socrates can explain away our wonder at the mutability, the sameness and the difference of things around us. The only true wonder Socrates would allow would be if the forms themselves — the things that truly *are* — could partake of opposites such as sameness and difference in themselves. Then, of course, the confusion that before we faced when considering terrestrial things would strike us when we contemplate the forms, and we could never be sure that our speech was true. This young Socrates is still something of a natural scientist. He equates wonder with confusion, and his goal seems to be to shape human speech into a precise representation of what he imagines truly *is*, the ideal.[10]

Why, in particular, is Socrates bent on this project, this conquest of confusion and profession of truth? We can find at least a beginning of an answer in his responses to Parmenides about what he believes qualifies as having forms. He believes that there are forms of such relational ideas as likeness and unlikeness. He is eager to admit forms of the just, the noble or beautiful and the good.[11] But he cannot decide whether there are forms of such beings as man, fire and water. And he emphatically denies the existence of forms of things like hair, mud and dirt (130b-130d). Socrates is not worried about rendering precise our speech about corporeal entities such as fire, water, mud or even man. His responses show in fact that he takes the formal existence, and pre-

---

[10] One may compare the picture Aristophanes gives us in his *Clouds*, 662 ff., where he makes Socrates try to rework the Greek language in laughable ways in order to fit his ideas of what is natural or true. See *Aristophanes Clouds*, translated with introduction and notes by Jeffrey Henderson (Focus Classical Library, 1992), pp. 53-55.

[11] In Greek the word *kalos* means both noble and beautiful.

eminence, of man an unquestioned starting point. Given man and his excellence, Socrates wants to understand and make clear precisely those matters wherein man's excellence — and his confusion — are most present and pressing: political matters. As the philosopher Aristotle will later say, "Fire burns both here and in Persia, but what's called Just is seen to differ."[12] Socrates has invented and wants to perfect political science.[13]

Socrates' zeal for speeches and his special interest in political things may be noble, but, as Parmenides emphasizes, it is lacking. Socrates' concern for politics is too political; it is tied to unquestioned and unquestioning common opinion. What characterizes Socrates' idea of forms most of all is his division of the intellectual or moral sphere from the physical or natural sphere, and the corresponding elevation of the former over the latter. This is a prejudice we meet quite frequently in our everyday speech, in our insistence that ideas are not reducible to atoms, that virtue is not a matter of genes, and that, above all, the soul is separate from and superior to the body. But our everyday speech is not so single-minded; it does not speak with one voice. We also recognize that without food, there's no thinking. And when we believe that someone has a wicked soul, what do we do often but call for his corporeal punishment — even death? Socrates is right to marvel at the confusion of common opinion and common speech. He is quite wrong, however, to establish one, partial opinion — namely, the belief in the duality of the intellectual and physical "worlds" — as the foundation of his inquiry into political matters. Let us recall Parmenides' passion, his insistence that to know the whole is to know it as one. Parmenides will not let young Socrates rest satisfied with what one element of conventional opinion says is to be honored and to be ignored. To move from particular or partial cares to concern for the whole as one is what it means for "philosophy to take hold" (130e).

Still, as the rest of the dialogue shows, to stop paying attention to conventional opinions about honor or worthlessness is not the only correction that Socrates needs. Socrates turned to forms, as we saw, because if there is a single and separate form for each thing, then by carefully defining each form we can render our speech about all things precise, powerful and true. The forms are meant to explain. But what is the point of Parmenides' conversation with young Socrates? That the forms themselves, the things that Socrates wants to explain everything else — these things themselves are inexplicable! Not only can we not explain how the beings among us come to partake in these

---

[12] *Nicomachean Ethics*, V.7.2. A serviceable translation is that of Rackham (Loeb Classical Library, 1926), p. 295. See also the forthcoming translation by William Cobb (Focus Philosophical Library).

[13] Parmenides too recognizes that Socrates' real interest is in politics. When he proposes his gymnastic he singles out the "noble or beautiful, just and good" as examples of the forms that Socrates has tried too soon to define (135c9).

mysterious forms (130e4-133a10), but the imagined remoteness of the world of forms — a separation needed to make them truly explicative of visible things — renders them powerless in our world and unknowable to the human mind (133c3-134c3). In short, positing these separate forms as the only true beings makes education nearly impossible and severs that Divine and Hyperborean world, the world of truth, completely from our perceptible world (see 133a11-c2, 134c9-135b2 and 134c4-139c8). Socrates' attempt to explain away our confusion has raised our wonder to a new level. And yet this impasse does not at all mean that he, or Parmenides, advocates abandoning the forms. Indeed, as Parmenides himself emphasizes, without the forms the understanding will be lost and the power of conversation destroyed. The Whole must be One, yet we can begin to make sense of it only by making it Two — and then, alas, that very attempt at explanation reveals itself to be insufficient. By "fleeing" to speeches, Socrates is stuck with wonder, wonder about the highest things, whether he likes it or not.

A Worklike Game

Such is the dilemma that young Socrates, and we with him, face as Parmenides proposes his "gymnastic," which he calls "a worklike game." But how in the world does what follows, that long and strange conversation between Parmenides and Aristotle, help us? All that Parmenides says is that if you do not practice it, "the truth will escape you" (135d6).

Perhaps the gymnastic consists in memorizing this entire conversation verbatim. This is certainly how Pythodorus, Antiphon and Cephalus took it — and all the better for us that they did! Yet Socrates does not appear to have taken it that way; at least we never see him later in life rattling off parts or the whole of this argument. In fact, he avoids, for the most part, abstract conversations that bear any resemblance to this one. Secondly, Parmenides explicitly mentions that the subject of this gymnastic can vary. One need not choose the One; rather one might take Likeness and Unlikeness, Motion and Rest, Genesis and Corruption, or even *Being* and *Not-being* (136a-b). Verbatim memorization would render impossible such variation. Finally, whereas Socrates became the philosopher par excellence, we cannot say the same about those who memorized this conversation. Pythodorus, the man who taught Antiphon the story, became an Athenian general active in Sicilian affairs, a signator of the Peace of Nicias and a violator of that same treaty. He also was exiled from Athens for a time for supposedly not conquering Sicily when he had a chance.[14] Later in his life Socrates comments that Pythodorus paid Zeno 100

---

[14]See Thucydides' *War of the Athenians and the Peloponnesians* III.115.2, V.19.24, VI.105, IV.65.3. See the translation by Smith (Loeb Classical Lib rary, 1919).

minae (the equivalent of several years' worth of college tuition today) to become "wise and famous."[15] Antiphon, as we learn from this very dialogue, left behind philosophical studies to spend his time with horses. And Cephalus, though we know very little of him, must have come to philosophy only late in life, and, if his wanderings are any indication, probably spent most of his life as a merchant of some sort (see 126b3). He does not call himself a philosopher, but acts as a guide for some fellow Clazomenians whom he calls "quite the philosophers" (126b8). Surely anyone who memorizes and can recite this amazing conversation proves himself able to do seriously hard work, but he does not thereby make himself a philosopher or obtain the truth.

If the gymnastic is not meant for memorization, maybe it is meant to teach some lesson that we need to learn? Our dilemma concerns the status of the forms. Are we then to take Parmenides' "One" as an abbreviated way of saying, "the Form, which is one"? Are all the arguments that follow deductions from the unity of Form? To take the conversation this way does yield interesting results and makes the forms even more wondrous. For example, we would learn from the first speech of the first argument that the One Form, which we want to use to judge the wholeness or partiality of something that we see, is itself neither a whole nor a part (see 137c-d). And the second speech would teach us that the Form, whose "look" we see in the shape of visible things, itself has no shape (see 137d-e). Taking the arguments this way clearly upsets all our imaginations about the forms. But again, we must remember that Parmenides advocates using this gymnastic on subjects other than the One, subjects which could not easily be taken as abbreviated ways of talking about Form in general. Also, to take the conversation this way is to limit the One, without any grounds but that we would like it to be so, to mean the One Form. Would we not then make the same error that Socrates made in his choice of what kind of forms to talk about? Would we not be limiting the One to what we think is most honored, rather than allowing it its full and universal sense? Finally, if this conversation is, in truth, a veiled lesson about forms, then it strangely had little or no outward effect on Socrates' own presentation of his forms later in life. In dialogue after dialogue he speaks about forms, especially the politically important ones. If this conversation somehow affected Socrates' own understanding of forms, it did so without making him change his presentation of them.

Let us return, then, to the surface of the conversation between Aristotle and Parmenides. Most obvious is the collision of two opposites: gravity and levity. Parmenides and Aristotle talk about the highest matters — the One, Sameness, Otherness, Time, Being — but they do so in what often appears to

---

[15] *Alcibiades Major* 119a. A translation of this dialogue is forthcoming by William Cobb (Focus Philosophical Library).

be a very silly way, and all their conclusions contradict one another. (Remember again, if you will, that last paragraph.) The gravity of the objects of conversation irresistibly demands that we piece together some serious teaching from this silliness. Is the levity then mere appearance or deception? For example, perhaps the gymnastic is in truth an exercise in logic, designed for young students in order to teach them how to separate "good" arguments from "bad" ones. If we are careful and logical, can we arrive at a hidden yet true teaching?

These are serious questions, yet we must remember that, if anything, by calling this conversation a "worklike game" (137b2) Parmenides denotes that what is serious about it is just the surface and that the play's the thing. Parmenides never hints that the conversation is meant as an exercise in logic or sleuthing. Furthermore, to chop up the dialogue and to take only a part of the whole as the truth would seem to violate most rudely Parmenides' own conviction that whatever truly *is*, is a unified whole. To ferret out a secret teaching from only part of this conversation would be as groundless, one could say, as what interpreters do when they take only half of Parmenides' own poem, the Way of Truth, as solely true and the rest as lies. Parmenides' teaching, if anything, is that any twofoldness or duplicity (which is the source of all other multiplicity), must be held together by the mind as One, if we are to know anything.[16]

But putting aside this hermeneutical politeness to Parmenides, we find that it is very difficult to say which arguments in this conversation are entirely "good" or "bad." Some do, to be sure, sound better than others, but none are wholly convincing nor wholly dismissable. It is for this very reason that the contradictions that result are truly puzzling. For example, at one point in the dialogue Parmenides asks Aristotle if the One has come into being against its own nature or not. Aristotle of course replies that it must have come into being in accordance with its nature. If, then, the One by nature is the totality of the whole, of which all these other things are parts, then the One, this universal whole, can only come into being last of all things: for only at that time will it be complete and hence truly One (see 153c-d). However, if each of these various things that comes into being before the universal One is, in fact, "each," then each of these is one and hence the One by nature must come into being at the same time as the very first of them (153d-e). The One, then, is both younger than and the same age as all the different things. Neither argument is bad, yet they clearly contradict one another.

A second example might make the difficulty of choosing "good" from "bad" arguments even more obvious. When talking about the One that *is* not, Parmenides notes that he and Aristotle are in fact talking about this hy-

---

[16]On duplicity in the *Parmenides* see Jacob Klein's "Note on Plato's Parmenides," in *Lectures and Essays*, edited by Williamson and Zuckerman, St. John's Press, 1985.

pothetically non-existent One. This One must, therefore, somehow partake of Being. For when we say that something "*is* not" — and we do say it and people understand what we mean —, we tacitly acknowledge that even something that *is* not partakes of *being*, namely *being* something that *is* not. If the non-existence of such a thing were truly unconstrained by this slender connection to Being, then we could not even conceive of it or speak of it (161e-162b). Non-being, after all, neither comes to be nor passes away: it *is*. However, the simplest sense of something's *not-being* is that it does not partake — no way, no how — in Being: it *is* not. From this point of view, to say that what *is* not partakes of Being is to speak nonsense. The One that *is* not, therefore, both partakes and does not partake of Being.

The reader can discern at this point that what changes from one argument to the next is not the quality of the logic, but the assumptions prior to the logic. The One of the very first argument above is the One imagined as the totality of all things, the most complete Whole. The second argument imagines the One as the unity of each individual thing which, even though a part of something else, we call "each" and therefore "one." The contradictions, and hence the apparent levity of this conversation do not derive from faulty logic, but from the continual shifting of unspoken assumptions.

Where does this observation leave us? Let us remember our earlier discussion of Zeno and his contradictions: if he wanted to prove the arrow moves, he would imagine time was continuous; when he wanted to call it motionless, he would imagine time was composed of indivisible instants. So is Parmenides just manipulating Aristotle (and us) by the old bait-and-switch? Or is he so inept that he does not even realize that he continually changes his assumptions about the hypothesized One? It seems hardly probable that Plato spent the time to compose this lengthy dialogue in order to present Parmenides as a shameful manipulator or total fool. If that were the case, there would be nothing serious in the dialogue — and what is left over would be a tasteless and very boring joke!

Perhaps we must conclude, then, that while Parmenides seems to speak about one hypothesis, namely the One, in fact his hypothesis changes every time his assumptions about it do. We would say, for example, that his hypothesis in the first argument (137c-142a) is that the One is only one (and nothing else, including existent), while in the second argument (142b-155e) he changes to a new hypothesis, that the One is both one and existent. This would be a serious attempt to make sense of the whole, but one that, to paraphrase Socrates' wry characterization of Zeno's speeches, "makes the One as Many as the arguments about it." Would not this explanation — that whereas he says he is going to speak about the One, he in fact speaks about many ones — also make Parmenides out to be a trickster or a fool? Again our serious efforts to understand it turn the dialogue into a terribly bad joke.

At last we are led, I believe, to conclude that neither the levity nor the gravity of the surface can, in truth, be separated off and discarded: they are one. The highest things, such as the One, defy precise representation by or in human speech. Each time you think you have it, you are in truth leaving something out. Or, to put it another way, whenever you try to speak about the One or other such things, you necessarily import certain turns of speech, certain assumed images of the thing you are talking about, imaginations which confound your apprehension of the intelligible. Mixing together the corporeal (your imagistic speech) with the intelligible, you attain only a partial statement about the thing itself. The conclusions you derive from what you imagine to be one sense of the One are therefore partial and conflict with those which you can derive from another. These are the lessons in humility that the proud, young, political scientist Socrates needs to learn. We must remember that Parmenides calls this gymnastic a "worklike game." We mortals are caught somewhere between the particularities of visible phenomena and the wholeness of the intelligible forms. At best our speech about these intelligible things, then, is playful; after all, true and precise knowledge of them, if there is such a thing, is the preserve of the gods alone. Our playful speech cannot serve as the firm foundation for a science of Being (ontology), mastery of which would turn men into gods. Parmenides' arguments with Aristotle are a majestic symphony of sorts, exploring every variation of our most comprehensive and most playful attempt at speech, our speech about the One. We must ask, therefore, whether in this dialogue Plato has surreptitiously undone the work of the historical Parmenides and has left us once again with nothing but the ever-wandering opinions of mortals.

Once again, from the Beginning

The young Socrates whom Parmenides meets at the beginning of this dialogue is a young man with passions that we can readily recognize in many young people. He is eager to get somewhere, to achieve clarity on the most important issues, to make some sense of things, especially political things. Whether his zeal has a selfish motive, to make a name for himself, or a philanthropic one, to improve his city, we do not know, nor is it important. Whatever his motive, Socrates wants to make progress.

Parmenides' response to this youth is that he must "draw back" and train in this gymnastic while he is still "young" (see 135d). Then, at the beginnings of almost all of the arguments which follow in his conversation with Aristotle, Parmenides repeats the phrase that heads this section: "Once again, from the beginning."[17] It is a command that Socrates respects (his first words

---

[17]He says these exact words at the beginning of arguments two, six and eight and he repeats nearly the whole phrase at four and seven. Of course, at the beginning of arguments one and five he is at the beginning, for he starts at those two places with the hypothesis itself.

in this dialogue are his request to Zeno to hear "once again" the "first" hypothesis) and many times in his later life we hear Socrates repeat these same words, "Once again, from the beginning."

How does this phrase characterize Parmenides' gymnastic, this gymnastic that he advises young Socrates to practice lest the truth escape him? The arguments themselves are characterized by chains of reasoning, some very long. But they always start again from the beginning, from the hypothesis itself and its inherent complexities. The syllogistic motion notwithstanding, the gymnastic teaches the student to eschew progress as usually understood. This gymnastic does not teach us to take the simplest and most important things as known and from there to build science upon them, as Descartes does in his *Rules for the Direction of the Mind* and as all mathematicians do with their axioms. Instead we learn from practice to return continually to these "simplest" things and to contemplate the complexities inherent in them. It is a labor of love, of the passion to know the whole as one and never let it go. The *Parmenides* is a most startling and most playful presentation of the union of mathematical deduction and division with poetic comprehensivity and completeness. The only "progress" here is a progress in our knowledge of our own ignorance about the highest things; or a progress in our knowledge that we cannot "hold together," in *logos*, the manifold truth of the highest things.[18]

We saw above that the historical Parmenides may be considered the man who began philosophy. From Plato's Parmenides we learn that philosophy, for it to be philosophy, must always return to its beginning. Being and the Forms — we must hypothesize their being, or else our understanding and our speech is lost. But we cannot explain how the things we see and speak about, the particular things, are one, in a whole, with these things which truly *are*. We cannot provide an account, both comprehensive and discursive, of the interrelation between the material and the divine "worlds." We cannot provide what Parmenides' hypothesis that "One *is*" reminds us we must try to provide: an account of how what seems to be two worlds is, in truth, one. Poetic or imagistic speech tries its best to encompass the whole. We may speak of the "material" versus the "divine" world. We may speak of particular things "partaking" or "participating" in the "forms." (Who taught Socrates to distinguish "forms" from particular things? He does not tell us, but perhaps the true teacher is the student, the poetic Plato.) But such poetry cannot answer the philosopher's questions. Philosophical speech and philosophical *eros* re-

---

[18]Can we, then, apprehend the truth in any way? Perhaps, as Plato hints, for brief "instants" as when a spark leaps from a fire (*Seventh Letter*, 341c). If so, it is not via speech that we do this, but, through, so to speak, "the eye of the soul," *nous*. N.B. that young Socrates' third and central attempt to explain the participation of things in forms is based on *nous* (132b3-c11).

main, as we learn in the *Symposium*, a daemonic intermediary between our perceptions and the truth. But it can keep this privileged, and playful, position only if it remembers always to return to its beginnings, to the complexities found in even the most simple speeches such as, "One *is*." Thus the *Parmenides* itself takes us back to the beginning, and in it we meet a "young" Socrates, a Socrates who, by never straying from the beginning, stays young for the rest of his long life.

Selected Bibliography

Allen, R.E. *Plato's Parmenides*. University of Michigan. 1983. A good analysis of the aporetic character of the whole of the dialogue (with translation).

Brumbaugh, R. "The Purpose of Plato's *Parmenides*." *Ancient Philosophy*. Fall 1980, vol. xlv. pp. 39-47. Provides an overview of previous theories about the dialogue's purpose and explicates *Parmenides* as pointing to the importance of *noesis*, in addition to *logos*, for philosophy. See also his *Plato on the One*. Yale. 1961.

Cherniss, H.F. "The Philosophical Economy of the Theory of Ideas." *American Journal of Philosophy* 57. 1936. pp. 445-456, reprinted in *Plato: A Collection of Critical Essays*. edited by G. Vlastos. Anchor Press. 1971. pp. 16-27. A powerful defense of the importance of Socrates' "ideas."

Cornford, F. *Plato and Parmenides*. London. 1939. A challenging and systematic account, filled with historical and technical information.

Miller, M. *Plato's Parmenides*. Princeton. 1986. A thorough attempt to make sense of the hypotheses and the dramatic purpose of the whole.

Proclus. *Commentary on Plato's Parmenides*. translated by G. Morrow and J. Dillon. Princeton. 1987. The classic neo-platonic commentary on the dialogue.

Rosen, S. *Plato's Symposium*. 2nd edition. Yale. 1986. The preface to this edition contains a most splendid and insightful discussion of the *Parmenides*.

Sinaiko, H. *Love, Knowledge and Discourse in Plato*. University of Chicago. 1965. The chapter on the *Parmenides* provides a careful reading of the hypotheses and an energetic account of the strength and weakness of speech.

Translator's Note

The translation is based upon Burnet's edition of the *Parmenides* (Oxford Classical Texts, 1901) with favor given to some divergent readings in Moreschini's more recent edition (Bibliotheca Athena, 1966).

As I noted above (note 1) I italicize the "existential" uses of the verb "to be" to distinguish them from the copulative. I also use italics to distinguish among translations of the forms of the noun "being," which though varied in Greek, appear nearly indistinguishable once translated into English. "Being" and "Non-being" (not italicized but capitalized) translate the Greek τὸ ὄν and τὸ μὴ ὄν, while "beings" translates the plural, τὰ ὄντα. "Beinghood," on the other hand, always translates οὐσία. "*Being*" and "*not-being*" (both italicized) translate the articular nominative forms of the verb "to be," namely, τὸ εἶναι and τὸ μὴ εἶναι. Finally, "to come into being" is often the translation of the Greek verb γίγνεσθαι, which in everyday speech can also have the connotation, "to be born." I have done my best to stick to these usages, so that the reader is not faced with more confusion than is already present in the dialogue itself.

Parmenides

(Or On Ideas: Logical)[1]

The Persons of the Dialogue:

Cephalus, Adeimantus, Antiphon, Glaucon, Pythodorus
Socrates, Zeno, Parmenides, Aristotle

126a   When we came to Athens from our home, from Clazomenae,[2] we chanced upon both Adeimantus and Glaucon in the market. And Adeimantus took me by the hand and said, "Welcome Cephalus! If you need anything here that's in our power, just say it."[3]

"Well, in fact," I replied, "I am here for this very thing: I need to ask you for something."

"Please tell us what you need," he said.

b   And I answered, "Your half-brother by your mother — what was his name? I can't remember. For surely he was just a boy, when I came from Clazomenae to stay here before. And it's been a long time since

---

[1] See Diogenes Laertius' *Lives of Eminent Philosophers*, III.57 and III.49 ff. about the notes that begin each Platonic dialogue and tell us something about their content and classification. The *Parmenides* is the only dialogue "On Ideas"; the *Statesman*, *Cratylus* and *Sophist* are also "logical" dialogues.

[2] Clazomenae was located on the west coast of Asia Minor and was one of the Ionian "dodecapolis," twelve cities which the Greeks, under the leadership of Athens, settled in archaic times. One famous son of Clazomenae was the philosopher Anaxagoras, who moved to Athens at the time of Socrates' youth and taught that *Nous* or Mind was the cause of all things.

[3] Glaucon and Adeimantus were Plato's brothers and play a large role in the *Republic*. Another Cephalus, a resident of Athens, also appears at the beginning of that dialogue.

23

then! But his father — I believe Pyrilampes was his name."

"Ah, yes," he said, "and his own was Antiphon. But why in the world do you ask?"[4]

"These men," I said, "are fellow citizens of mine and quite the philosophers. They heard that this Antiphon spent much of his time with a certain Pythodorus, a companion of Zeno. And that those speeches **126c** which Socrates and Zeno and Parmenides once made in conversation — that Antiphon heard them so many times from Pythodorus that he has them memorized."

"That's the truth," he said.

"Well," I replied, "this is what we need — to hear them through-and-through."

"Oh, that's no difficulty," he said. "For when he was a boy he practised them quite well, thoroughly. But nowadays, just like his grand-father of the same name, he spends much of his time on horsemanship. But if it's necessary, let's go to him. For he only just left here for home, and his house is nearby in Melite."[5]

127a   This said, we started walking and came upon Antiphon at home, handing a bridle-bit or something to a smith to fit. Once he'd freed himself of that fellow and the brothers began to tell him why we were there, he recognized me from my previous stay and greeted me warmly. We then asked him to go through the speeches. At first he balked — for he said it was a lot of work — but at last he led us through them in full. And so Antiphon said that Pythodorus used to say that both Zeno and Parmenides once came to the Great Panathenea.[6]

b   Now, Parmenides was already quite old — his hair all white — but the vision of a gentleman.[7] He was sixty-five at most. Zeno was then nearly forty, tall and pleasing to look at. (He was said to have been

---

[4]   Pyrilampes was Plato's step-father and, as a descendant of a noble family and a friend of Pericles, was active in Athenian politics of the later fifth century. Antiphon, therefore, was younger than Plato, Glaucon and Adeimantus.

[5]   Melite was a particular "deme" or political subdivision of Athens, in which was located many of the city proper's most famous places, including the Acropolis.

[6]   A Panathenea was celebrated in mid-summer every year to honor the birth of Athena and the "synoecism" or unification of Athens. Every four years the citizens held a much larger festival, with parades and contests, called the "Great Panathenea."

   The reader should remember that what follows, though it appears in dra-matic 'real-time,' is all part of Cephalus' trebly indirect narration.

[7]   A "gentleman," in Greek, is literally someone who is both "beautiful (or noble) and good."

Parmenides' young beloved.) They were staying, he said, with
127c Pythodorus outside the city-wall in the Potter's Quarter.[8]

So Socrates and many others with him went there, since they de-
sired to hear Zeno's writings — after all, that was the first time they had
brought them there. Socrates was then very young. Zeno himself read
to them, but Parmenides chanced to be out. And there was, all-in-all,
only a short part of the speeches left to be read, Pythodorus said, when
he and Parmenides with him came in from outside — and Aristotle too
(who became one of the Thirty).[9] So they heard only a little of the
writings. However, Pythodorus, in fact, had heard them before on his
own from Zeno.

After listening, Socrates asked him to re-read the first hypothesis
of the first speech. Once it was read he said, "Zeno, how do you mean
that? If the things that *are*, are many, then, according to you, they must
be both like and unlike. But this is clearly impossible, since the unlike
cannot be like nor the like unlike. Isn't that what you mean?"

"That's so," replied Zeno.

"And so if it is impossible for the unlike to be like and the like
unlike, it's also impossible for there to be many things? For if there
should be many, they would suffer these impossibilities. Is this, then,
what your speeches seek — nothing else than to battle against everything that is commonly said by maintaining that there *is* no many? And
do you think that each of your speeches is a proof of this very thing —
so that the supposed proofs that 'There *is* no many' are as many as the
128a speeches you have written? Is that what you mean, or don't I understand you right?"

"No," said Zeno, "on the contrary, you have beautifully grasped
the whole of what my writing seeks."

"I'm coming to understand, Parmenides," Socrates said, "that
Zeno here seeks to be your partner not only in friendship but in writing! For he has written, in a certain way, the very same thing as you, but
by changing it around he tries to trick us into thinking that he is saying
some other thing. You in your poems say that All is one, and you do a

---

8   The "Keramikos" or Potter's Quarter was a location north-west of the city
    which was home also to many of Athens' finest burial sites. The Panathenaic
    procession started there.

9   The Thirty Tyrants (led by Plato's uncle Critias) took control of Athens in
    July 404 B.C. after her defeat by the Spartans in the Peloponnesian War.
    Their short but bloody reign of terror was ended in January 403 B.C. by the
    moderate oligarchs. The Thirty were all executed at that time or in the years
    following. One must remember that this Aristotle is *not* the same as the
    great fourth-century philosopher, the student of Plato.

128b both beautiful and good job of proving that; but this fellow, in turn, says that it's not many, and he offers proofs that are very many and very great. One says 'The One' and one says 'Not Many,' and so each speaks so as to seem to say nothing the same, while you are saying nearly the same thing. That's why what you say appears to be over the heads of the rest of us."

"Yes, Socrates," said Zeno. "But you have not perceived the entire truth of my writing. To be sure, you both chase and hunt down

c what I said like a Laconian hound! But this much has escaped you from the first: that in no way whatsoever is my writing so pretentious as to have been written for the reason you offer, namely, to conceal from men that it's furthering some great plot. What you mentioned is just an accidental result. The truth is that it's a sort of aid to Parmenides' speech against those who attack him by joking that if one *is*, then he and his

d speech suffer many laughable and contradictory results. So this writing refutes the asserters of the Many and pays back the same and more. It seeks to make this point clear: that if sufficiently prosecuted, their hypothesis — 'If many *is*' — would suffer even more laughable results than that of the One's *being*. I wrote it, in fact, when I was young, because I loved to fight. But someone stole a copy, so I couldn't decide

e whether it should be brought to light or not. That's what escapes you, Socrates: you don't think it was written because of a youth's love for fighting, but because of an older man's love of honor. Though, as I said, your description is not a bad likeness."

"I accept that," replied Socrates, "and I believe it is as you say. But tell me this: don't you think that there exists, in itself, some form[10]

129a of Likeness, to which is opposed a different one, which is unlike, and that both you and I and the different things which we do in fact call 'many' come to partake of these two things which *are*? And that the things that come to partake of Likeness become like in both the manner and extent that they partake, but those of Unlikeness unlike, and those of both, both? And even if all things come to partake of both these opposing things and are, by partaking in both, both like and un-

b like in themselves — why wonder? For if someone were to show that the like things themselves become unlike or the unlike like, I'd think that a marvel. But if he shows that whatever partakes of both of these has experienced both, then, Zeno, it doesn't seem at all out of place to me. No, not even if he were to show that all things are one by partaking of the One and that these same things are many, in turn, by partaking in Multitude! But if he demonstrates that whatever one is, this very thing,

---

[10] This is the first appearance of Socrates' famous "forms." For more on young Socrates and the forms see the introduction.

is many and that the Many, in turn, are one — of course I'll wonder at
129c that. Likewise for all the different things: if he should reveal that both
the kinds and forms themselves experience these opposite experiences
in themselves, it's right to wonder. But if someone demonstrates that I
am one and many, why wonder? For when he seeks to show that I am
many, he just mentions that my right is one thing and my left another,
my front's one thing and my back's another, and likewise for upper and
lower — for I do, I believe, partake of Multitude. But when he wants to
d show that I am one, he'll say that out of the seven of us who are here, I
myself am one man and partake of the One. So he can show that both
are true.

"If, then, someone shall try to show that for things such as stones
and wood and the like, the same things are many and one, then we will
say that he's demonstrated that some thing is many and one, not that
the One is many or the Many's one. He's not even said anything wondrous, but only what in fact all of us should readily agree upon. But if
someone, as I just said, shall first distinguish the forms as separate in
themselves, such as Likeness and Unlikeness and Multitude and the
e One and Rest and Motion and all the like, and then will show that in
themselves these things can be mixed together and separated, I'd ad-
mire that with wonder, Zeno!" he said. "Now I do believe that you've
worked over these things quite bravely; but, as I've said, I would ad-
mire this much more: if someone could demonstrate that even in the
130a forms themselves — in the things grasped by reasoning — there is ev-
erywhere tangled up that same impasse which you proved is present in
the things we see."

While Socrates was speaking, Pythodorus said, he himself thought
that at each word both Parmenides and Zeno were going to get angry.
But they kept their mind on Socrates and, with frequent glances to one
another, they smiled as if admiring him. Which is, in fact, what
Parmenides told him, once he was done.

b   "Socrates," he said, "you ought to be admired for your zeal for
speeches! And tell me, did you, on your own, come up with this division that you speak of between these forms, separate unto themselves,
and, separated from them, the things that partake of them? And does it
seem to you that Likeness itself is separate from the likeness that we
possess? And so on with one and many and everything that you heard
of just now from Zeno?"

"It certainly does," answered Socrates.

"Well how about these sorts of things," said Parmenides, "such
as a form of Justice in itself and of Beauty and of Good and so on?"

"Yes," he said.

130c   "But what about this: a form of Man separate from us and all those like us — some very form of Man, or of Fire or Water?"

"I've hit a dead end many times, Parmenides," he replied, "over these, over whether it's necessary to speak much the same about them or differently."[11]

"Well then, Socrates, what about those things that would seem to be laughable, such as Hair and Mud and Dirt or any different thing that's very worthless and lowly? Are you at an impasse over whether it is or is not necessary to say that there is a separate form of each of these, d   something different than what we can lay our hands on?"

"No, not at all!" answered Socrates. "For these things are as we see them right here, and it would be grossly out of place to think that there is some form of them. To be sure, it has troubled me that the same case does not apply to all, but whenever I come to this, I run off, fearing to fall and perish in some abyss of foolishness. In the end, then, I return to these things that just now we were saying are forms and I spend my time working over them."

e   "Well, you are still young, Socrates," said Parmenides, "and philosophy has not yet grabbed you as it will, in my opinion. Then you will dishonor none of these things; but as for now, you still look to the opinions of men, because of your age. But tell me this, then: does it seem to you that, as you say, there are these forms from which the different things here, by partaking in them, get their names? For example, the things that partake in Likeness become like, but those in 131a   Greatness great, and those in Beauty and Justice both just and beautiful?"

"Of course," replied Socrates.

"And so each thing that partakes comes to partake either of the whole form or of a part? Or could there be some way of partaking separate from these?"

"How could there be?" he said.

"Then does it seem to you that the whole form is in each of the many things, while still being one, or how?"

"What prevents it, Parmenides," said Socrates, " from being one?"

b   "Although one and the same, then, its whole will be in many

---

[11] The word here translated "dead end," and sometimes "impasse," is *aporia*, the state of "being-at-a-loss" or without anywhere to turn that the older Socrates is famous for always claiming to be in and to lead others into (see *Meno* 80a-d).

separate beings at the same time, and so it would be separated from itself."

"Not if it is like a day," he said, "which, although one and the same, is many places at once and is not at all separate from itself. In this way each of the forms could be one, the same and in all things at once."

"Socrates," he replied, "how nicely you make one and the same thing many places at once! It is as if after covering many men with a sail you would say that it is one whole over many. Or is this not what you mean to say?"

131c   "That's fair," he answered.

"Well then would the whole sail be over each man, or a different part of it over each different man?"

"A part."

"Then, Socrates," he said, "the forms themselves can be partitioned and the things that partake of them would partake of a part. The whole would no longer be in each, but each would possess a part."

"So it appears."

"Well then Socrates, are you willing to say that one form can, in truth, be partitioned by us and still be one?"

"No way," he replied.

d   "Try to see then," he said, "if you'll partition Greatness itself, then each of the many great things will be great by means of a part that's smaller than Greatness itself — doesn't that appear illogical?"

"Of course," he answered.

"But what? If something possesses an individual small part of the Equal, will it possess something that, though less than the Equal itself, will make its possessor equal to anything else?"

"Impossible!"

"Then let one of us possess a part of the Small. Since it's just a part, the Small will be greater than it. Get it? — the Small itself will be

e   greater! But whatever that subtracted piece is added to will be smaller, not greater, than before!"

"Well that certainly can't be," he said.

"Is there, then, some other way, Socrates," he asked, "that the different things will partake of your forms, since they're able to partake neither as parts nor as wholes?"

"No by Zeus!" he exclaimed. "It doesn't seem to me to be at all easy to determine that!"

"But what then? How do you feel about this —"

"What's that?"

132a   " — I think that you think that each form is one because of this: whenever many things seem to you to be great, it seems probable to you, as you look over them all, that there *is* some one and the same idea. From this you conclude that the Great is one."

"That's the truth," he replied.

"But what about the Great itself and the different great things — if, in the same way, you look over them all with your soul, will there not appear, in turn, some great thing that makes all of them, by necessity, appear great?"

"It looks that way."

"A different form of Greatness, then, will be revealed, in addition to what was Greatness itself and the things that partake of it. And above all of these, in turn, another, that makes them all great. And so each of b your forms will no longer be one, but will be boundless in multitude."

"But Parmenides," Socrates said, "couldn't it be that each of these forms is a thought and properly comes to *be* nowhere but in souls? Then each could in fact be one and would not still suffer the things you just mentioned."

"What then?" he asked. "Each is one of our thoughts — but are there thoughts of nothing?"

"Impossible," he replied.

"So of something?"

"Yes."

c   "Of something that is or is not?"

"That is."

"So of one thing — which thing in fact the thought thinks is present in all cases as some one idea?"

"Yes."

"Then won't a form be this thing that is thought to be one, since it's always the same in all cases?"

"It appears necessary."

"But what now?" asked Parmenides. "For doesn't it seem to you that, since it is necessary, you say, for other things to partake of forms, either each thing consists of thoughts and everything thinks or, although thoughts, they're thought-less?"

"Well that too," he replied, "makes no sense. However,

132d Parmenides, here's how it really appears to me to be: these forms stand in nature like patterns. The different things resemble them and are likenesses, and so the different things' participation in the forms turns out to be nothing else than to be made in their likeness!"

"If then," he asked, "something looks like a form, can the form not be like its likeness, insofar as that thing's been made like it? Or is there some trick that can make the like be like what's not like it?"

"No, there isn't."

"But doesn't a great necessity force the like, along with the thing
e like it, to partake of one and the same form?"

"Necessarily."

"But whatever the like things are like by participating in — isn't that the form itself?"

"Entirely so."

"Nothing, then, can be like the form nor can the form be like anything else. Otherwise there will always appear a different form be-
133a yond the form; and if that is like anything, another still. And there will never be an end to the genesis of new forms as long as the form becomes like the thing that partakes of it."

"That's most true."

"It's not by likeness, then, that the different things come to partake of forms. Instead it's necessary to seek a different way of partaking."

"It looks that way."

"Do you see then, Socrates," he asked, "how great an impasse lies before anyone who tries to determine that there are forms in themselves?"

"Very much so!"

"And so know well," he said, "that you have, so to speak, not
b even touched upon how great an impasse there is if you try to posit each form as one, somehow distinguishing them from the beings."

"How's that?" he replied.

"There are many different reasons," he answered, "but here's the greatest. If someone should argue that the forms themselves — should they be as we say they must be — cannot, properly speaking, be known, no one could prove to whomever argues this that he's mistaken, unless the one arguing chanced to be experienced in many things and not naturally dull. This person would have to be willing to follow the fellow working over the proof through many cases and over a long distance,

133c otherwise he who forces them to be unknowable would be persuasive."

"Why's that Parmenides?" asked Socrates.

"Because, Socrates, I think that both you and anyone else who posits that there's a certain beinghood in itself for each thing would first agree that none of them *are* among us."

"How could it still be 'in itself' then?" replied Socrates.

"Beautiful," he said. "And so all those ideas that are what they are relative to one another have their beinghood relative to themselves and not in relation to the things among us — whether likenesses or, how-
d ever one posits them, what we partake of and from which, then, we are called by certain names. The things among us, then, these things which take the forms' names, are themselves related only to themselves, but not to the forms, and they belong only to themselves and not to whatever things are named the same."

"How do you mean that?" asked Socrates.

"Here's an example," said Parmenides. "If one of us is a master or a slave of someone, he is not, of course, a slave to what Master itself
e is, nor is the master a master of what Slave itself is. Instead, since he's a man, he's both of these to another man. For Mastership itself is what it is of Slavery itself, and likewise Slavery itself is slavery to Mastership itself. The things among us have no power in relation to those things, nor they to us; instead, like I said, those things belong to themselves and are in relation to themselves and so too the things among us to
134a themselves. Or do you not understand what I mean?"

"Oh, I understand well," replied Socrates.

"And so also knowledge. Would what Knowledge itself is," he asked, "be knowledge of what Truth itself is?"

"Of course."

"But then what each branch of knowledge is would be knowledge of what each of the beings is, or no?"

"Yes."

"But wouldn't the knowledge among us be of the truth among us; and, in turn, each branch of knowledge among us would have to be
b knowledge of each of the beings among us?"

"Necessarily."

"And yet the forms themselves, as you agree — neither do we possess them nor could they *be* among us."

"No, they couldn't."

"But surely what each of the kinds themselves is, is known by that very form, the form of Knowledge?"

"Yes."

"Which we certainly don't possess."

"No, we don't."

"None of the forms, then, is known by us, since we don't partake of Knowledge itself."

"It doesn't look that way."

"Then what the Beautiful itself is and the Good and all the things
134c that we do suppose to be ideas are unknown to us."

"I'm afraid so."

"See then something still more terrible than this!"

"What's that?"

"You would probably say that if there *is* in fact a certain kind itself of Knowledge, it is far more precise than the knowledge among us, and the same for Beauty and all the rest."

"Yes."

"And so if anything else does partake of Knowledge itself, wouldn't you say that god, more than anyone else, possesses this most precise knowledge?"

"Necessarily."

d   "Then will the god, in turn, be able to know the things among us, since he possesses Knowledge itself?"

"Why not?"

"Because," said Parmenides, "we agreed, Socrates, that whatever power they do have, those forms have no power relative to the things among us, nor the things among us relative to them. Instead, each group relates only to themselves."

"Yes, this was agreed."

"And so if the god possesses this most precise Mastership and this most precise Knowledge, then their mastership could never master us,
e nor could their knowledge know us or anything else of the things among us. Likewise, we do not rule over them by the authority among us, nor, by our knowledge, do we know anything of the divine. According to this speech, in turn, they are not our masters nor do they know anything of human affairs — since they are gods!"

"But what an altogether wondrous speech, if it strips the god of knowing!"

"Nevertheless, Socrates," said Parmenides, "the forms must, by

135a necessity, have these problems and many more still, if there are these ideas of the beings and if one distinguishes each form on its own. The result is that whoever hears this hits a dead end and argues that these things *are* not; and if, at most, they should *be*, well, then, great necessity keeps them unknown to human nature. And while he says these things this fellow will even seem to be talking sense and, as we said before, he will be wondrously hard to convince. Only a naturally gifted man could learn that there is a certain kind and beinghood, in itself, for

b each thing; and only a still more wondrous person will discover all these things and be able teach someone else to judge them clearly and sufficiently for himself."

"I agree with you, Parmenides," Socrates said. "To my mind, you speak well."

"And yet," said Parmenides, "if someone, in turn, Socrates, after focusing on all these problems and others still, shall deny that there are forms of the beings and will not distinguish a certain form of each single thing, wherever he turns he'll understand nothing, since he does

c not allow that there is an ever-same idea for each of the beings. And so he will entirely destroy the power of dialogue. But you seem to me only too aware of this."

"That's the truth," he replied.

"What then will you do about philosophy? Where will you turn if all this is unknown?"

"At present, at least, I can't seem to see."

"It's because, Socrates," he said, "you are trying too soon, before being trained, to define some Beautiful and Just and Good and

d each one of the forms. I noticed this even the day before yesterday when I overheard your conversation with this fellow Aristotle. Know well: that zeal which drives you towards speeches is beautiful and divine. But you must draw yourself back and train more, while you're still young, in a gymnastic that seems useless and which the many call 'idle talk.' If you don't, the truth will escape you."

"What's the manner, Parmenides," he asked, "of this gymnastic?"

"It is what you heard just now from Zeno," he replied. "Except

e for this, in fact, I really admired you when you were speaking to him, because you wouldn't investigate this perplexity among the visible things nor even in reference to them, but only in reference to what most of all one should grasp by speech and consider forms."

"That's because," he replied, "this way, there seems to me no difficulty in showing what beings are like and unlike and experience anything else."

"Beautiful," he said. "But, in addition, you must do this: do not only investigate the results of a hypothesis if each hypothesized thing *is*, **136a** but also hypothesize that this same thing *is* not. Do that, if you want to get more gymnastic training."

"What do you mean?" he asked.

"Take, if you like," he said, "this hypothesis that Zeno hypothesized: 'If many *is*, what must result both for the Many themselves in relation to themselves and in relation to the One and for the One both in relation to itself and in relation to the Many?' Then, in turn, if many *is* not, you must inquire what will result both for the One and the Many both in relation to themselves and in relation to each another. And yet **b** again, if you'll hypothesize, 'If Likeness *is*' or *is* not, what in the case of each hypothesis will be the result both for the very things hypothesized and for the different things both in relation to themselves and in relation to each other? And it's the same speech for Unlikeness and Motion and Rest and Generation and Corruption and even *being* itself and *not-being*. In a word, whatever you hypothesize about, whether it *is* or *is* not and whatever other experience it suffers, you must always investi- **c** gate the results in relation to itself and in relation to each one of the different things, whichever you chose — in relation both to many and to all of them, likewise. And, in turn, whether you hypothesize that what you have hypothesized *is* or *is* not, you must investigate these different things both in relation to themselves and in relation to whatever else you choose, if you intend, after being completely trained, to attain a lordly view of the True."

"It's quite an impossible task, Parmenides, that you're talking about, and I don't really understand it. But why don't you hypothesize something and go through it for me, so that I can understand better?"

d "Why, that's a lot of work, Socrates," he replied, "to demand from a man my age!"

"Well then you," said Socrates, "Zeno — why don't you go through it for us?"

And Zeno, he said, said laughing, "Socrates, let's ask Parmenides himself, since it's not, as he says, a trivial thing. Or don't you see how much work you're demanding? If there were more of us, it wouldn't be right to ask. For it's unseemly, especially for someone of his age, to **e** speak such things before the many, since the many do not know that without this digressing and wandering through all things it is impossible to possess a mind that's hit upon the True. And so Parmenides, I join Socrates in asking, that I may also listen after all this time."

Now once Zeno said that, Antiphon said that Pythodorus said that he and Aristotle and the others asked Parmenides to do nothing else than to demonstrate what he meant. Then Parmenides said, "Necessary it is to obey. And yet I seem to be suffering something like that Ibyceian horse, which, as a prizewinner but old, is about to take part in a chariot race and, being experienced, trembles at what is about to happen. Ibycus says that he resembles the horse since, although he is so old and unwilling, Necessity forces him to fall in love.[12] And so I seem quite fearful, since I remember what sort of and how great a multitude of speeches I must swim through at my age. Nevertheless, I must show you this favor, especially since, as Zeno says, we are by ourselves.

b   "So where will we start and what will we hypothesize first? Or, since now it seems I must play at this worklike game, shall I begin with myself and my hypothesis, that is, hypothesizing about the One itself, whether one *is* or one *is* not, what must result?"

"Of course," said Zeno.

"Who then," he asked, "will answer me? How about the youngest? He would be the least trouble and would say exactly what he thinks. And, at the same time, his answers would give me some time to relax."

c   "I'm ready for you, Parmenides," said Aristotle. "For you mean me if you mean the youngest. Just ask and I'll answer."

So be it, he said. If there's one, then the One could in no way be many?[13]

---

[12] Ibycus was a late sixth century lyric poet who lived in Italy. The poem referred to here was saved by the scholiast to the *Parmenides* (see Ibycus 287 in Page's *Poetae Melici Graeci*). A literal translation of the whole follows:

> "But Eros, gazing at me from under
> Dark eyelids, melting me with his eyes,
> With all sorts of charms does he drive me
> Into the inescapable nets of Kypris.
> O yes, I do tremble going in,
> Just as a horse, yoked up, a prizewiner but old,
> Unwillingly goes to contend with swift chariots."

[13] This is the first hypothesis and argument: One is. In it Parmenides deduces what the results of the hypothesis will be for the One itself. The argument extends from here, 137c4, to 142a7. To help the reader keep track of where he is in this ocean of words, I have included a Roman numeral at the head of each page that denotes which argument is going on (for a synopsis of all eight see the introduction, p.5). I also note at the head whether Parmenides is deducing results from the hypothesis for "one" or for "Different things," and I offer a brief indication of what subject in particular he is discussing

How could it?

So it must neither have a part nor be a whole.

Why's that?

Surely the part is a part of a whole —

Yes.

— But what is the whole? Wouldn't a whole be whatever lacks no part?

Of course.

So in both cases the One would consist of parts — if it were a whole or if it had parts.

Necessarily.

Then in both cases, likewise, the One would be many and not one.

137d   True.

But surely it must be one, not many.

It must.

Therefore it will neither be a whole nor have parts — if the One will be one.

It won't.

And so, if the One has no part, it would have neither beginning nor end nor middle. For such things would then be its parts.

Right.

And yet beginning and end are certainly a limit to each thing.

How not?

Then the One is limitless, if it has neither beginning nor end.

Limitless.

e   And without shape, therefore: for it partakes of neither round nor straight.

How's that?

Well round, of course, is that whose extremities on every side hold off equally from the center.

Yes.

(e.g. rest, motion, likeness, unlikeness, etc.). This concise system should help the reader follow the arguments as well as compare Parmenides' various treatments of particular subjects amid all eight major arguments.

And straight, then, is whose middle is in front of both extremities.

That's so.

And so the One would have parts and would be many, if it should partake of either a straight or round shape.

Of course.

Therefore it's neither straight nor round, since, in fact, it has no parts.

138a   Right.

Furthermore, since it's of this very sort, it would not be anywhere. For it wouldn't be either in anything else or in itself.

How's that?

Well, if it were in anything else, surely it would be surrounded in a circle by whatever it's in and would be touched by its many parts in many places. But since it is one and partless and does not partake of **b** circularity, it's impossible for it to be touched on many sides in a circle.

Impossible.

And likewise, should it be in itself, it would surround itself by nothing else than itself — if it could, in fact, be in itself. For that something be in something that doesn't surround it, is impossible.

Impossible.

And so the thing surrounding would be one thing and the thing being surrounded another, since a whole, of course, will not both suffer and do the same thing at the same time. And thus the One would not still be one but rather two.

It wouldn't.

Therefore the One is not anywhere — neither being in itself nor in anything else.

No, it isn't.

See then if, being this way, it is able to stand at rest or be in motion.

Well, why couldn't it?

Because, if it were in fact in motion, either it would go some-**c** where or it would change. For these are the only motions.

Yes.

But should the One change from itself, it's surely impossible for it still to be one.

Impossible.

So it isn't moved by change, at any rate.

It appears not.

But by going somewhere?

Perhaps.

And yet if the One goes somewhere, either it goes around in the same place in a circle or it exchanges one place for another.

Necessarily.

And so, should it go around in a circle, it must have a middle as a base and various parts, parts of itself, that go around the middle. But **138d** since it properly has neither middle nor parts, is there some trick to make it go around the middle in a circle?

None at all.

Then surely, should it change place, it comes to be in one place from another and so is in motion?

If in fact it is, at any rate.

That it be anywhere in anything — wasn't this shown to be impossible for it?

Yes.

Then it is even more impossible for it to come to be?

I don't understand why.

If something is coming to be in something, isn't it necessary that, while it is still coming to be therein, it not yet be in it and yet not be still entirely outside it — if, in fact, it is already coming to be therein?

Necessarily.

e   If, then, anything else suffers this, it could only be something that has parts. For a certain part of it would already be in the thing, but at the same time part of it would be outside. But whatever has no parts will certainly be unable, in any way, either to be inside or outside of something, as a whole, all at once.

True.

And whatever has no parts nor chances to be a whole — wouldn't it be still more impossible for it to come to be anywhere, since it could come to be therein neither by parts nor as a whole?

It appears.

Then neither by going anywhere and coming to be in something
139a does it change place, nor by revolving in the same place, nor by changing.

It doesn't look like it.

Thus as regards every motion, the One is motionless.

Motionless.

And, furthermore, we say that it is impossible for it to be in something.

We do say this.

So then it is never in the same thing.

Why's that?

Because it would already be in that thing which is the same.

Of course.

But it was able to be in neither itself nor another.

No, it wasn't.

And so the One is never in the same thing.

It looks like it isn't.

b   Well, then, since it is never in the same thing, it's never at peace
nor does it stand at rest.

No, it couldn't.

The One, then, so it looks, neither stands at rest nor is in motion.

To be sure, it appears not.

Nor will it be the same as another or as itself, nor, in turn, would
it be other than itself or another.

How's that?

Should it be somehow other than itself, it would be other than
one and would not be one.

True.

And, in addition, should it be the very same as another it would
c be that thing, but would not be itself. So, again, it would not be what,
in fact, it is — one — but rather other than one.

No, it wouldn't.

It won't, then, be the same as another or other than itself.

No, it won't.

But it certainly won't be other than another, as long as it is one.

For one is not properly other than anything — only other, and nothing else, is other than another.

139d   Right.

So, by being one, it will not be other. Or do you believe it will?

Certainly not.

But if not by this, it won't be so by itself; but if not by itself, it won't be so. Since it is in no way other, it will be other than nothing.

Right.

Nor will it be the same as itself.

But how not?

The very nature of the One is surely not the same as of the Same.

Why's that?

Because whenever something becomes the same as something it does not become one.

Well, what then?

Should it become the same as the many, it would necessarily become many and not one.

True.

But if the One and the Same in no way differ, whenever something became the same, it would always become one; and whenever one, the same.

e   Of course.

If, then, the One will be the same as itself, it will not be one with itself. And thus, although one, it will not be one. But of course this is impossible. Therefore it is also impossible for the one to be other than another or the same as itself.

Impossible.

So the One clearly would be other or the same as neither itself nor another.

No, it wouldn't.

Nor will it be like or unlike anything, either itself or another.

Why's that?

Because whatever has somehow experienced the Same is like.

Yes.

But it was shown that the nature of the One is separate from the

Same.

140a   This was shown.

And yet if the One experienced something separate from being one, it would have experienced being more than one. But this is impossible.

Yes.

So there's no way, then, for the One to have experienced the same thing as anything else or itself.

It appears not.

It's not possible, then, for it to be like anything else or itself.

It doesn't look like it.

Nor has the One experienced being at all other; for this way it would have experienced being more than one.

Yes, more.

But whatever has had any sort of experience other than itself or anything else would be unlike itself or anything else, just as whatever **b** has experienced the Same is like.

Right.

But the very One, so it looks, having had no sort of other experience, is in no way unlike either itself or another.

No, it isn't.

Therefore the One would be neither like nor unlike either another or itself.

It appears not.

And, in addition, being of this very sort, it will be neither equal nor unequal to itself or anything else.

How?

Should it be equal, it will consist of the same measures as that to which it is equal.

Yes.

But should it somehow be greater or less, then, as concerns what**c** ever it is commensurate with, it will have more measures than the lesser things and less than the greater.

Yes.

But as concerns whatever it is not commensurate with, than some it will consist of smaller measures, than others, greater.

How not?

And so isn't it impossible for whatever doesn't partake of the Same to consist of the same measures or anything else whatsoever the same?

Impossible.

Then it would be equal neither to itself nor to anything else, since it would not consist of the same measures.

It appears not, to be sure.

Furthermore, should it consist of more or less measures, howsoever many are its measures, of so many parts would it consist. And so, **140d** again, it will no longer be one but rather as many as are the measures.

Right.

But if, in fact, it should consist of one measure, it would be equal to the measure. Yet this was shown to be impossible: that it be equal to anything.

This was shown.

Therefore, since it does not partake of one measure or many or few, and since all-in-all it does not partake of the Same, it will never be equal, so it looks, to itself or to anything else. Nor, again, will it be greater or less than itself or another.

Entirely so.

e   But what? Does it seem possible for the One to be older or younger or to have the same age?

Well, why not?

Because surely should it have the same age as itself or anything else, it will partake of Equality of time and Likeness — things which we said the One does not partake of, that is, either Likeness or Equality.

We did say that.

And, in addition, that it does not partake of Unlikeness and Inequality — we said this too.

Of course.

141a   How then will something of this sort be able to be older or younger than anything, or to have the same age as anything — since it's of this sort?

There's no way.

So then the One would neither be younger nor older nor have the same age as either itself or anything else.

It appears not.

Then would the One be unable to *be* in time in any way, if it should be of this sort? Or isn't it necessary, if something is in time, for it to be becoming ever older than itself?

It's necessary.

Now, isn't the older, in fact, always older than the younger?

What else?

141b So whatever becomes older than itself at the same time also becomes younger than itself — if, in fact, it is going to have something to become older than.

How do you mean that?

Like this: One thing cannot become different from another when it already is different; rather, since it already is, it must already be; and if it has become so, it must have become so; or if it's going to be so, it must be going to be so. But if it's becoming so, it must neither have become nor be going to be nor be different yet; rather, it must become so and nothing else.

c That's quite necessary.

But, to be sure, the older is a difference from the younger and nothing else.

It is.

Then whatever is becoming older than itself must necessarily at the same time also become younger than itself.

It looks like it.

But, of course, it cannot come into being more or less — in respect to time — than itself. Rather it must become and be and have become and be going to be for an equal time with itself.

These things too are necessary.

And therefore it is necessary, so it looks, for everything that is in d time and partakes of this sort of thing to be the same age, itself as itself, and at the same time to become both older and younger than itself.

I'm afraid so.

But surely the very One can partake in no such experiences.

No, it can't partake.

Therefore it has no share in time, and it *is* not in any time.

No indeed, just as the speech claims.

What then? Don't the was and the had-become and the was-becoming seem to signify participation in a time which has become?

Very much so.

141e   But what? Don't the will-be and the will-become and the will-be-made-to-become seem to signify partaking in a time going to be hereafter?

Yes.

And certainly the is and the is-becoming seem to signify partaking in the present time?

Of course.

If, then, the One in no way participates in any time, then it has never become nor was it becoming nor was it once, nor has it become now nor is it becoming nor is it, nor will it become hereafter nor will it be made to become nor will it be.

Most true!

Is there any way different than one of these for something to partake of beinghood?

There is not.

Therefore in no way does the One partake of beinghood.

It doesn't look like it.

So the One in no way *is*.

It appears not.

And so it *is* in no way so as to be one. For it would already be a thing and partake of beinghood. But, so it looks, the One neither is one nor *is* — if it's necessary to trust this very speech.

142a   I'm afraid so.

But whatever is not — could there be anything for it or of it, should it not be?

And how could there?

So, then, there's no name for it nor account, nor is there any knowledge of it nor perception nor opinion.

It appears not.

And, then, it's not named nor spoken of nor opined nor known, nor do any of the things that *are* perceive it.

It doesn't look like it.

Well, then, is it possible that this is the way it is concerning the One?

No, it sure doesn't seem so to me, at least!

142b   Do you want us then to go back up to the hypothesis once again from the beginning, in case something might appear different to us as we go back through it?[14]

I very much want to.

And so, if one *is*, we say that the results concerning it, whatever they chance to be, we must agree on them. Or is this not so?

Yes, it is.

Look then from the beginning: if one *is*, is it able to be and yet not to partake of beinghood?

No, it cannot.

And so the beinghood of the One would *be* while not being the same as the One. For otherwise it would not be its beinghood, nor c would it, the One, partake of it. Instead, to say that 'one *is*' and 'one is one' would be alike. But this is not now the hypothesis, 'If one is one, what must result,' but rather it's, 'If one *is*.' Or is this not so?

Of course it is.

And so the '*is*' signifies something else from the 'one?'

Necessarily.

Then whenever someone says, in short, that one *is*, would he be saying anything else than this — that the One partakes of beinghood?

Of course.

But let us ask again, if one *is*, what will result. Look into whether it isn't necessary for this hypothesis to signify that the One is of such a sort as to have parts —

d   How?

— Like this: If the '*is*' is said of the One which *is* and the 'one' of the beinghood that's one, but the beinghood and the One are not the same, and rather are said of that which we hypothesized — namely, of the One which *is*—, then isn't it necessary that a one that *is* be itself the whole, and that the One and the *being* come into being as pieces of this?

Necessarily.

---

[14] Now we begin the second argument. The hypothesis is still "One is," and once more Parmenides deduces the results for the One. But the results are the exact opposite of those in the first argument. This argument runs from 142a8 to 155e3. It is by far the largest of the eight, just a bit bigger than the other seven combined.

Then will we call each of these two pieces only a piece, or must the piece itself be called a piece of the whole?

Of the whole.

And, then, it's a whole, whatever is one, and has a piece.

Of course.

What then? Does each of these pieces of the One that is, the One 142e and Being, lack something? Does the One lack the piece that's the *being* or Being the piece that's the One?

They would not.

And so, again, each of the pieces holds fast to the One and Being, and the very least piece comes to consist, in turn, of two pieces, and, according to the same speech, it is always this way. Namely, whatever piece comes to be, it always holds fast to these two pieces; for the One always holds fast to Being and Being to the One. The result is that, since it always becomes two, it necessarily is never one.

143a   Entirely so.

And so the One that *is* would be limitless in multitude?

It certainly looks that way.

Come now, once more here.

Where?

Do we say that the One partakes of beinghood, therefore it *is?*

Yes.

And because of this, in fact, the One that *is* appears to be many.

That's so.

But what? The One itself, which, in fact, we say partakes of beinghood — if we grasp it with the understanding, alone by itself, without that which we say it partakes of, then, at least, will this same thing appear only one or also many?

One — that's what I myself believe.

b   Let us see then. It's necessary for its beinghood to be one thing, something different, and it another, if, in fact, the One is not beinghood but rather, as one, partakes of beinghood.

Necessarily.

And so if beinghood is one thing and the One another, then neither by being 'one' is the One other than beinghood, nor by being 'beinghood' is beinghood something different from the one, but by being other and different they are other than one another.

Of course.

So the Other is not the same as the One or as beinghood?

How could it be?

143c   What then? If we will choose whichever you like of them, either beinghood and the Other or beinghood and the One or the One and the Other, then in each choice don't we choose some two that could correctly be called 'both?'

How?

Like this: is it possible to say 'beinghood?'

It is.

And likewise to say 'one?'

This too.

Then haven't each of the two been spoken of?

Yes.

But whenever I say something is both beinghood and one, then don't I say both?

Of course.

And so too, if both beinghood and other or both other and one, and so in every way and in each case I speak of both?

Yes.

d   But whatever are correctly addressed as 'both,' is it possible for them to be both but not two?

It's not possible.

But whatever are two, is there some trick to make each of them not one?

None whatsoever.

Of these, then, — since in fact they all result in pairs —, each would be one.

It appears.

But if each of them is one, whenever any one whatsoever be added by any sort of yoke, don't they all become three?

Yes.

And isn't three odd and two even?

How not?

But what? Since there are two, isn't it necessary that there also be
143e twice? And since three, thrice — if in fact it is the case that two is twice
one and three is thrice one?

Necessarily.

But since there is two and twice, isn't it necessary for there to be
two twice? And since there's three and thrice, isn't it necessary, in turn,
for there to be three thrice?

How not?

But what? Since there's three and twice and two and thrice, isn't
it necessary that there be three twice and two thrice?

Very much so.

144a And so there would be even even-times and odd odd-times and
even odd-times and odd even-times.

This is so.

If, then, this is so, do you believe that there is any number left out
which doesn't have to *be* by necessity?

None at all.

If, therefore, one *is*, it is necessary for number also to be.

Necessarily.

And yet, if there is, in fact, number, there would be many things
and a limitless multitude of beings. Or doesn't number become limitless in multitude even while partaking in beinghood?

Of course it does.

And so if all number partakes of beinghood, would each piece of
number also partake of it?

Yes.

b Over all the many beings, therefore, is beinghood apportioned
and does it stand aloof from none of the beings, from neither the smallest nor the greatest? Or isn't it illogical even to ask this? For, really, how
could beinghood itself stand aloof from any of the beings?

There's no way.

So, then, it has been chopped up into the very smallest and greatest things and beings of all sorts, and it is by far the most partitioned of
all things, and there will be infinite parts of beinghood.

c That's the way it is.

Most numerous, then, are its parts.

Most numerous, of course.

What then? Is any of these things, which is a part of beinghood, nevertheless no part at all?

And how could this sort of thing come to be?

Well if, at any rate, I believe that there is, as long as it *is*, it must always, by necessity, be one thing; it's impossible that it be nothing.

Necessarily.

To every part of beinghood, therefore, the One is attached and is not lacking in either the smaller or greater parts or in anything else.

That's so.

Then, if one be many places at once, is it at the same time a whole?
144d Think about that.

Well, I'm thinking about it and I see that it's impossible.

It's been partitioned, then, if in fact it's not a whole. For in no other way, certainly, will it be present in all the parts of beinghood at the same time, unless it's been partitioned.

Yes.

And yet a great necessity forces whatever has parts to be as many as its parts are.

Necessarily.

Then we were not speaking the truth, just now, when we said that beinghood had been apportioned into the most numerous parts. For it had not been apportioned into more than the One, but rather into an
e equal number, so it looks, as the One. For Being neither lacks the One nor the One Being; rather, since they are two, they are always, in every case, equal.

It appears entirely so.

The One, therefore, having being chopped up by beinghood, is both many and limitless in multitude.

It appears.

Therefore, not only is the being that is one many, but even the One itself, since it has been divided up by Being, must, by necessity, be many.

Entirely so.

And yet, since the pieces are pieces of a whole, wouldn't the One have been limited by the whole? Or are pieces not surrounded by the whole?

145a   Necessarily they are.

But surely whatever surrounds would be a limit.

How not?

The One that *is*, then, is somehow both one and many, and a whole and pieces, and limited and limitless in multitude.

It appears.

Then since it is, in fact, limited, wouldn't it also have extremities?

This is necessary.

But what? If a whole, wouldn't it also have beginning and middle and end? Or could there be some whole without these three? And if any one of these shall stand aloof from something, will it still be able to be a whole?

It will not be able.

And so in fact it looks as though the One would have beginning
b and end and middle.

It would have them.

But surely the middle, at any rate, holds off equally from the extremities. For otherwise it wouldn't be a middle.

No, it wouldn't.

And so, should it be of this sort, it looks like the One would partake of some shape, whether straight or round or some mixture of both.

Yes, it would partake.

Since, then, this is the case, won't it be both in itself and in anything else?

How?

Surely each of the parts is in the whole and none is outside the whole.

That's so.

But all the parts are surrounded by the whole?

c   Yes.

And yet the One is all the parts, its parts, and is neither at all more nor less than all of them.

No, it isn't.

And so the One is also the whole?

How not?

If, then, all the parts chance to be in the whole and they are all the One and it is the whole, but they are all surrounded by the whole, then by the One would the One be surrounded, and so the One itself would already be in itself.

It appears.

However, the whole, at any rate, is not, in turn, in the parts, 145d neither in all nor in any. For if in all, it is necessarily also in one — since, should it not be in a certain one, still less could it be in all. If this one is among them all, and the whole is not in this, how will it still be present in them all?

There's no way.

But it's not even in some of the parts: for if the whole should be in some, then the more would be in the less, which is impossible.

Yes, impossible.

But should the whole not be in more nor in one nor in all the parts, isn't it necessary that the whole be in a certain other thing or else be nowhere?

e   Necessarily.

And so, since whatever is nowhere would be nothing, even if it's a whole, and since it is not in itself, isn't it necessary for it to be in anything else?

Of course.

Insofar, then, as the One is a whole, it's in something else. But insofar as it chances to be all those parts, it's in itself. And thus the One itself must, by necessity, be both in itself and in another.

Necessarily.

Since it is clearly of this nature, isn't it necessary that the One both be in motion and stand at rest?

How?

Surely it stands at rest, if in fact it is in itself. For, should it be in 146a one thing and not go away from this, it would be in the same thing, in itself.

Yes, it is.

But whatever is always in the same thing must, by necessity, without a doubt, always be standing at rest.

Of course.

But what? Since, in opposition, the One is always in another, it necessarily is never in the same thing. But since it's never in the same thing, it musn't stand at rest. And by not standing at rest mustn't it be in motion?

That's so.

It's necessary, therefore, for the One, since it is always both in itself and in another, always both to be in motion and to stand at rest.

It appears.

146b And, in addition, it must be the same as itself and other than itself, and likewise both the same as and other than the different things, if in fact it has also experienced those previous things.

How?

Surely everything is to everything else like this: either it is the same or other, or if not the same and not other, it would be a part of whatever it is thus related to or it would be as a whole is to a part.

It appears.

Then is the One itself a part of itself?

No way.

Nor, then, would it be a whole of itself, as to a part, as though being a part in relation to itself.

No, it wouldn't.

c   But is the One other than one?

Surely not!

Nor, then, would it be other than itself.

Certainly not.

If, then, it is neither other nor whole nor part in relation to itself, isn't it necessary for it to be the same as itself?

Necessarily.

But what? Isn't it necessary for whatever is in another place than itself (since itself is in the same place as itself) to be other than itself — if, in fact, it will be in another place?

It seems so to me, at any rate.

But, in fact, the One has been shown to be this way: it is at the same time both in itself and in another.

Yes, this was shown.

So it looks like, by this, the One would be other than itself.

146d   It looks that way.

What then? If something is other than something, won't it be other than whatever is other?

Necessarily.

And so all the things that are not one are other than the One, and the One is other than whatever is not one?

How not?

The One, then, would be other than the different things.

Other.

Look then: aren't the Same itself and the Other opposed to one another?

How not?

Well, then, will the Same ever be able to be in the Other or the Other in the Same?

They will not be able.

If, therefore, the Other will never be in the Same, then there is no being which the Other is in for any amount of time: for if it should be **e** in anything whatsoever, for that amount of time the Other would be in the Same. Or is this not so?

It's so.

But since it is never in the Same, the Other would never be in any of the beings.

True.

So the Other would be neither in whatever is not one nor in the One.

No, it wouldn't.

Then not by the Other would the One be other than whatever is not one, nor by it would whatever is not one be other than the One.

No, they wouldn't.

But surely not by themselves would they be other than one another, since they do not partake of the Other.

147a   How would they?

But if neither by themselves are they other nor by the Other, then wouldn't they, in every way, escape not being other than one another?

They would escape it.

And yet whatever is not one does not partake of the very One. For then it would not be not-one, but would somehow be one.

True.

Nor, then, would whatever is not one be a number. For by having number they would in no way be not-one.

No, they wouldn't.

But what? Are the things that are not one pieces of the One? Or wouldn't then the things that are not one partake of the One?

They would partake.

147b So if, in every way, something is one and other things are not one, then the One would neither be a piece of whatever is not one nor as a whole of pieces. Nor, in turn, could the things that are not one be pieces of the One, nor as wholes to the One as a piece.

No, they wouldn't.

And yet we said that whatever is neither pieces nor wholes nor other than one another will be the same as one another.

We did say this.

Shall we also say, then, that the One is this way in relation to the things that are not one: it is the same as them?

Let's say it.

The One, then, so it looks, is other than both the different things and itself and is the same as both them and itself. .

I'm afraid this appears to be the case from this very speech.

c Then also both like and unlike both itself and the different things?

Perhaps.

Since, at any rate, it was shown to be other than the different things, surely the different things would also be other than it.

Why, how not?

And just as it's other than the different things, so too would the different things be other than it — neither more nor less?

Well, what then?

If, therefore, neither more nor less, in a like way.

Yes.

And so, insofar as it has experienced being other than the different things and the different things likewise than it, in this way the One would have experienced the same thing as the different things and the different things as the One.

d How do you mean this?

Like this: don't you assign each name to something?

I do.

What then? Could you say the same name many times or once?

I could.

Then if you say it once do you address whatever possesses the name, but if you said it many times you don't address this thing? Or, whether once or many times you utter the same name, doesn't a great necessity force you always to mean the same thing?

Why, how not?

Now is the 'other' a name for something?

Of course.

147e   Whenever, then, you utter it — whether once or many times — you refer to nothing different nor name anything different than whatever in fact possessed the name.

Necessarily.

But whenever we say that the different things are other than the One or that the One is other than the different things we say the 'other' twice. Yet we always say it in reference to that nature which possessed the name.

Of course.

148a   Insofar, therefore, as the One is other than the different things and the different things than the One, then, by having experienced the Other itself, the One would have had no different experience than the different things, but rather the same. But surely whatever has experienced the same thing is like: or not?

Yes.

Yet, insofar as the One has experienced being other than the different things, for this same reason everything would be like everything. For everything is other than everything.

It looks that way.

And yet the Like, at any rate, is opposed to the Unlike.

Yes.

And so too, the Other to the Same.

This too.

And, in addition, this was shown as well: that the One (it seems) is the same as the different things.

b   Yes, it was shown.

But to be the same as the different things is quite the opposite experience of being other than the different things.

Of course.

Yet, insofar as other, it was revealed like.

Yes.

Insofar, then, as it's the same, it will be unlike, since it experiences the opposite of the experience that makes it like. For surely the Other made it like?

Yes.

The Same, therefore, will make it unlike, or it won't be opposed to the Other.

148c   It looks that way.

Therefore the One will be like and unlike the different things: insofar as it's other, like; but insofar as the same, unlike.

Yes, it looks, in fact, as though the speech is of this sort.

And it's also like this —

What?

— Insofar as it has experienced the same thing, it hasn't experienced something different; but whatever hasn't experienced something different is not unlike; and whatever's not unlike is like. But insofar as it has experienced something different, it's different, and whatever's different is unlike.

That's the truth.

Since the One, then, is the same as the different things and since **d** it's other, — as regards both and each — it would be both like and unlike the different things.

Of course.

And so likewise as regards itself: since, in fact, it was shown to be both other than itself and the same as itself, as regards both and each, will it be revealed both like and unlike?

Necessarily.

But what then? Look into what's the case concerning the One's touching and not touching itself and the different things.

I'm looking.

For surely the One itself was shown to be in itself as a whole.

Right.

And so too the One's also in the different things?

Yes.

Insofar, then, as it's in the different things, it would touch the **148e** different things. But insofar as it's in itself, it would be kept from touching the different things and it would touch itself, since it's in itself.

It appears.

So clearly the One would touch itself and the different things.

It would touch.

But what about this? Mustn't everything that's going to touch something sit next to whatever it's going to touch, thereby occupying that seat which sits beside that of the thing it touches?

Necessarily.

And the One, then, if it's going to touch itself, must sit right next to itself, thereby occupying that place connected to the one it is in.

Yes, it must.

And so, as though two, the One would do this and would come **149a** to be in two places at the same time. But as long as it is one, it won't be able to, will it?

No, it won't.

The same necessity, then, that makes the One not be two makes it not touch itself.

The same.

But neither will it, in fact, touch the different things.

Why's that?

Because, we say, whatever's going to touch, since it's a separate thing, must be next to whatever it's going to touch, and no third thing can be in the middle of them.

True.

There must be two things, then, at the very least, if there's going to be a touch.

There must.

But if to the two boundaries a third be added in succession, then **b** they will be three, but the touches two.

Yes.

And so, clearly, whenever one thing is added, one touch is also added and the result is that the touches are one less than the number of the multitude. For by an amount equal to that by which the first two

exceeded the touches (by being more numerous than the touches), so every future number of things will also exceed all the touches. For in
149c the future whenever one is added to the number of things, one touch will also be added to the touches.

> Right.

However many in number, then, are the beings, the touches are one less than they.

> True.

But if, in fact, there is only one thing, and no dyad, there would be no touch.

> How could there?

Now, we say that the things different than the One are neither one nor do they partake of it — if indeed they are different.

> No, they don't.

There is, then, no number in the different things, since the One is not in them.

> How could there be?

The different things, then, are not one nor two nor anything that
d has the name of a different number.

> No.

The one alone, then, is one, and there could be no dyad.

> It appears not.

There is, then, no touch, since there are no two things.

> No, there isn't.

The One, therefore, does not touch the different things nor the different things the One, since, in fact, there is no touch.

> No, they don't.

So, clearly, in accordance with all this, the One both touches and does not touch the different things and itself.

> It looks that way.

Then is it both equal and unequal to both itself and the different things?

> How?

If the One should be greater than the different things or less, or
e if, in turn, the different things should be greater or less than the One, then not by being one nor by being different than the One would the

One and the different things be at all greater or at all less than one another — that is, not by these, their very beinghoods —, would they? Instead, if, in addition to being of this sort, each should possess Equality, they would be equal to one another. But if the different things possessed Greatness and the One Smallness, or the One Greatness and the different things Smallness, then wouldn't whichever form Greatness was present in be greater, and wouldn't whichever Smallness was present in be less?

Necessarily.

And so are there, in fact, these two forms — Greatness and Smallness? For surely if there were not, they would not be opposed to one another and would not come to be present in the beings.

150a   How could they?

If, then, Smallness became present in the One, it would be there either in the whole or in a part of it.

Necessarily.

But what if it should become present in the whole? Wouldn't it either have been stretched equally throughout the whole of the One, or surround it?

Obviously.

Then, should it be equal throughout, wouldn't Smallness be equal to the One itself; and, should it surround it, it'd be greater?

How not?

Then is it possible for Smallness to be equal to something or greater than something and so do the work of both Greatness and Equality and
b not its own work?

Impossible.

So Smallness could not be in the whole of the One; instead, if at all, it's in a part.

Yes.

But it cannot, in turn, be in an entire part, otherwise it will do the same things it did in respect to the whole: it will be equal or greater than whatever part it would ever be present in.

Necessarily.

Smallness, then, will never be present in any of the beings, since it cannot come to be therein either in a part or in a whole. And nothing will be small except Smallness itself.

It doesn't look like it.

Nor, then, will Greatness be present in anything. For then some-
150c thing different and separate from Greatness itself would be greater —
namely, whatever Greatness is present in. And this even though there's
no small in it, which it must by necessity exceed, if in fact it's great. But
this is impossible, since Smallness is present nowhere.

True.

Furthermore Greatness itself is not greater than anything else than
Smallness itself, nor is Smallness less than anything else than Greatness
itself.

No, it's not.

The different things, then, are neither greater nor less than the
One, since they partake of neither Greatness nor Smallness. Nor do
d these two have in relation to the One any power of exceeding or being
exceeded, but only in relation to one another. Nor, again, could the
One be greater or less than these two or the different things, since it
partakes of neither Greatness nor Smallness.

It certainly appears not.

Then if the One is neither greater nor smaller than the different
things, isn't it necessary for it neither to exceed nor be exceeded by
them?

Necessarily.

Now, a great necessity makes whatever neither exceeds nor is exceeded be on equal terms, and it makes whatever is on equal terms
equal.

How not?

e   And, to be sure, the One itself is this way in relation to itself: since
it possesses neither Greatness in itself nor Smallness, it could not be
exceeded by nor exceed itself; instead, by being on equal terms it would
be equal to itself.

Of course.

The One, then, would be equal to both itself and the different
things.

It appears.

And yet since it is, in fact, in itself, it would also be around itself
from without; and by surrounding itself it would be greater than itself,
151a but by being surrounded, less. And thus the one itself would be greater
and less than itself.

It would.

Now, is this also necessary: that there is nothing outside the One and the different things?

How not?

But surely whatever in fact *is* must always be somewhere?

Yes.

And so whatever is in something will be in the greater, since it's less? For otherwise one thing would not be in another.

No, it wouldn't.

But since there is nothing other separate from the different things and the One, and they must be in something, isn't it now necessary for them to be in one another — the different things in the One and the **151b** One in the different things —, or else be nowhere?

It appears.

Because, then, the One is present in the different things, the different things would be greater than the One (since they surround it), and the One would be less than the different things (since it is surrounded). But because the different things are in the One, the One, according to this speech, would be greater than the different things and the different things less than the One.

It looks that way.

The One, then, is itself both equal to and greater and less than both itself and the different things.

It appears.

And, in addition, if in fact greater and less and equal, it would consist of equal and more and less measures than itself and the different **c** things, and since of measures, also of parts.

How not?

Then by consisting of equal and more and less measures, in number it would be less and more than both itself and the different things and also equal to both itself and the different things in this same respect.

How?

Than whatever it is in fact greater than, it would surely consist of more measures — and as many as are the measures, so also the parts. And for whatever it is less than, likewise; and for whatever it is equal to, the same.

That's so.

And so, since it is greater and less and equal to itself, wouldn't it **d** consist of equal and more and less measures as itself, since of the measures, so also of the parts?

How not?

Since, then, it consists of equal parts as itself it would be equal in multitude as itself; but since it consists of more parts, it would be more in number than itself; and since of less, less.

It appears.

And so won't the situation be the same for the One in relation to the different things? Since it appears greater than they, it is necessary that it also be more than they in number. But since it appears smaller, less; and since it appears equal in greatness, is it necessary that it also be equal in multitude with the different things?

It's necessary.

151e In turn, so it looks, the One itself will thus be equal and more and less in number than both itself and the different things.

It will be.

Does the One, then, also partake of time, and is it and does it become both younger and older than both itself and the different things and also neither younger nor older than itself or the different things, by so partaking of time?

How?

Surely *being* is in it, if in fact one *is*.

Yes.

But is *being* anything else than participation in beinghood along with the present time, just as the 'was' is a community with beinghood 152a along with the past, and, in turn, the 'will be' is such along with the future?

Yes, it is.

Then it partakes of time, if in fact it partakes of *being*.

Of course.

Now, of a time that's advancing?

Yes.

It always becomes older than itself, then, if it goes forward in time.

b Necessarily.

Do we remember that, while becoming younger, the older becomes older?

We remember.

And so, since the One becomes older than itself, would it become older than itself while it's becoming younger?

Necessarily.

So clearly it is becoming both younger and older than itself.

Yes.

But it is older, isn't it, whenever it is coming to be in the time now, the time between the 'was' and the 'will be'? For surely while advancing from the once to the hereafter it will not overstep the now.

No, it won't.

152c At that time, then, won't it hold off from becoming older, since it has chanced upon the now, and it no longer becomes but already is, at that time, older? For while going forward it was never held fast by the now. For whatever goes forward is able to touch upon both of these — the now and the hereafter — this way: by letting go of the now and seizing the hereafter as it comes to be between them both, that is, the hereafter and the now.

True.

But unless, in fact, it's necessary for everything that becomes to circumvent the now, then whenever it's in it, it will always hold off d from becoming and will be, at that time, whatever it chanced to be becoming.

It appears.

And the One, then, whenever by becoming older it chances upon the now, it holds off from becoming and is, at that time, older.

Of course.

And so, whatever it was becoming older than, of this it is older. But was it becoming older than itself?

Yes.

And the older is older than the younger?

It is.

And the One, then, is younger than itself at that time when, by becoming older, it chances upon the now.

Necessarily.

e But the now, surely, is always present in the One throughout all of its *being*. For it is always 'now' whenever in fact it *is*.

How not?

The One, then, always both is and becomes older and younger than itself.

It looks that way.

And is it or does it come to be for more time than itself, or for an equal time?

Equal.

And yet whatever becomes or is for an equal time has the same age.

How not?

But whatever has the same age is neither older nor younger.

No, it's not.

The One, then, since it both becomes and is for an equal time as itself, is and becomes neither younger nor older than itself.

It doesn't seem so to me.

But what? Than the different things?

I can't say.

153a   Surely you can say this at least: that the things different from the One, if in fact they are others and not an other, are more than one. For whatever is an other would be one; but since they are others, they are more than one and would possess multitude.

Yes, they would possess it.

And whatever is a multitude would partake of a number more than one.

How not?

What then? Will we say that, of number, the more both come to be and have come to be first, or the less?

The less.

b   The very least, then, is first: and this is the One. Isn't it now?

Yes.

Of all the things that have number, then, the One came to be first. But all the different things also possess number, if in fact they are different things and not a different thing.

Yes, they do possess it.

But, I believe, by coming to be first it came to be previously, and the different things later. But whatever things came to be later are younger than what came to be previously, and so the different things would be younger than the One, but the One would be older than the different things.

Yes, it would be.

But what about this: could the One have come into being against
153c nature, against its own nature, or is that impossible?

Impossible.

Yet surely the One was shown to have parts, and, if parts, then
also a beginning and end and middle.

Yes.

And so of all things — of both the One itself and each of the
different things — does a beginning come into being first, and after the
beginning all the different things until the end?

Why, how not?

And, in addition, we will say that all these things, the different
things, are in fact pieces both of the whole and of one, and that it itself
became both one and whole at the moment of the end.

Yes, we'll say this.

But I, at any rate, believe an end comes into being last of all, and
d the One, by nature, comes into being at the same time as this thing. So
that, if it is in fact necessary for the One itself not to come into being
against nature, then by having come into being at the same time as the
end, it would by nature come into being last, after the different things.

It appears.

The One, then, is younger than the different things and the different things are older than the One.

So, in turn, it appears to me.

But what then? A beginning or any different part of the One or of
any different thing, if indeed it is a part and not parts, isn't it necessary
for it to be one, since it's a part?

Necessarily.

And so the One would come into being at the same time as the
e first thing that comes into being, and at the same time as the second,
and it's not missing from any of the different things that come into
being, since in fact it's added to any of them that comes to be one
whole by reaching its extreme end. Neither from the middle nor from
the first nor from the extreme end nor from any different thing in genesis is it missing.

True.

The One, then, maintains the same age as all the different things. So if the One hasn't grown, by nature, against nature, it would have come into being neither before nor after the different things, but at the same time. And, according to this speech, the One would be neither older nor younger than the different things, nor the different things than the One. But, according to the previous one, it would be both older and younger, and the different things likewise than it.

Of course.

Clearly it is this way and has come to be this way. But what, in turn, about its becoming both older and younger than the different things and the different things than the One, and their becoming neither younger nor older? Just as it is for *being*, is it this way also for becoming, or is it other?

I can't say.

Well I can say this: even if one thing is older than another, it could not become any older than by however much it differed in age when it first came into being; nor, in turn, should it be younger, it could not become any younger. For whenever equals be added to unequals, both in time and in anything else, they always make the difference equal to however much differed at first.

How not?

Being, then, could never become older or younger than the One that *is*, if in fact they always differed equally in age. For it is and has become older, and the other one younger — they are not coming to be so.

True.

And the One that *is*, then, never becomes either older or younger than the different things which *are*.

No, it doesn't.

But see if there's any way for them to become older or younger.

What way's that?

Inasmuch as the One was shown to be older than the different things and the different things than the One.

What then?

Whenever the One is older than the different things, surely it has come into being for more time than the different things.

Yes.

Consider it again: if to more and to less time we shall add an equal amount of time, will the more differ from the less by an equal piece or by a smaller one?

By a smaller one.

Then however much the One differed in age at first from the different things, there will also be this difference afterwards; but as it accrues time equally with the different things, it will always differ less in age from them than before. Or not?

Yes.

154e   Now, whatever differs less in age in relation to something than before would become younger than before in relation to whatever previously it was older than?

Yes, younger.

But if it is becoming younger, aren't those different things, in turn, becoming older than before in relation to the One?

Of course.

Whatever had come to be younger, then, is becoming older in respect to whatever previously both had come to be and was older. But it never is older; instead, it is always becoming older than the other. For the latter advances towards the younger, and the former towards the older. Likewise, in turn, the older is becoming younger than the younger. For as they go in opposite directions they are becoming opposites of one another: the younger is becoming older than the older and the older younger than the younger. But they cannot 'became.' For if they became, they would not still be becoming; rather, they'd be. But now they are becoming older than one another and younger: The One is becoming younger than the different things, since obviously it is older and came into being first; and the different things are becoming older than the One, since they came into being later. But according to the same speech, the different things also are this way in relation to the One, since, in fact, they are obviously older and came into being first.

155a

b

Yes, it's obviously this way then.

And so, insofar as no one thing comes to be older than another or younger, because they always differ from one another by an equal number, then neither could the One become older than the different things or younger, nor the different things than the One. But insofar as — by an ever different piece — it is necessary for whatever came into being before to differ from what's later and whatever came into being later to differ from what's before, then for this very reason is it necessary for them to be becoming older and younger than one another, namely, the different things than the One and the One than the different things?

c

Of course.

So according to all of this, the One itself both is and becomes older and younger than both itself and the different things, and neither is nor becomes either older or younger than either itself or the different things.

Completely so.

155d But since the One partakes of time and of becoming both older and younger, isn't it necessary for it also to partake of the once and the hereafter and the now — if in fact it partakes of time?

Necessarily.

The One then was and is and will be and was becoming and becomes and will become.

Why, how not?

And should there be anything to it and of it — this thing was and is and will be.

Of course.

And clearly there would be knowledge and opinion and perception of it, if in fact we are now doing all these things concerning it.

You're right!

And clearly there's a name and a definition for it, and it's named **e** and spoken of, and whatever else of this sort chances to apply to the different things also applies to the One.

That's the case — completely.

Let's now speak yet a third time. The One, if it is as we have described it — isn't it necessary for it (since it is both one and many and being neither one nor many and partaking of time), since one *is*, sometimes to partake of beinghood, but since it *is* not, sometimes, in turn, not to partake of beinghood?[15]

Necessarily.

Then while it partakes will it be able, at that time, not to partake? Or when not partaking, to partake?

---

[15] What follows, up till 157b5, is sometimes treated by commentators as the third argument, thus bringing the total number of arguments up to nine. I do not take it to be a new arguement, since Parmenides does not repeat the basic hypothesis, something he does in all eight arguments, but rather he takes the One "as we have described it," sc. in argument two. This section, then, is probably an appendix to arguments one and two.

It won't be able.

At one time, then, it partakes and at a different time it does not partake: for this is the only way it could both partake and not partake of the same thing.

156a   Right.

And so is there also the time when it comes to partake of *being* and when it lets go of it? Or how will it be able at one time to have and then not to have the same thing, unless it at one time takes and then releases it?

There's no way.

But surely you call coming to partake of beinghood becoming?

I do.

And isn't letting go of beinghood perishing?

Yes, of course.

The One, then, so it looks, by both taking and releasing beinghood, both comes to be and perishes.

b   Necessarily.

But since it is one and many and coming to be and perishing, then whenever it becomes one, doesn't the 'being many' perish, and whenever it becomes many, doesn't the 'being one' perish?

Of course.

But in becoming one and many, isn't it necessary that it be both divided and collected?

Very much so.

In addition, whenever it becomes unlike and like, musn't it be made both unlike and like?

Yes.

And whenever it becomes greater and less and equal, mustn't it be both increased and diminished and made equal?

That's so.

c   But whenever from being in motion it stands at rest, and whenever from standing at rest it changes to being in motion, surely it itself must not be in one place in time.

How's that?

If at first it stands at rest and later is in motion, and if at first it's in motion but later stands at rest, it won't be able to suffer such things without changing.

How could it?

But certainly there is no time at which something could at once neither be in motion nor stand at rest.

No, there isn't.

And yet it doesn't change without changing.

Not likely.

When, then, does it change? For it changes neither when it stands at rest nor when it's in motion nor when it is in time.

156d   No, it doesn't.

Is there, then, this out-of-place thing that it would be in, at that time when it changes —

What sort of thing?

— The instant. For the 'instant' looks like it signifies this very thing: something from which there is a change in either of two directions. For while still standing at rest something cannot change from standing at rest; nor while still in motion can it change from motion. Instead this sort of momentary, out-of-place nature lurks between both

e motion and rest and is not in any time. Thus, into this and out of this, whatever's in motion changes to standing at rest and whatever stands at rest changes to being in motion.

I'm afraid so.

And the One, then, if in fact it both stands at rest and is in motion, would change from each of these two — for this way is the only way it could do both —, but changing it changes in an instant, and when it changes it would be in no time, nor would it at that time be in motion or stand at rest.

No, it wouldn't.

Then is it also this way in relation to the other changes? When-

157a ever from *being* to perishing it changes, or from *not-being* to becoming, doesn't it at that time come to be between both these motions and rests, and neither is at that time nor is not, neither becomes nor perishes?

It certainly looks that way.

According to this speech, then, when going from one to many and from many to one, it is neither one nor many, neither is it separated nor collected. And when going from like to unlike and from unlike to like, it's neither like nor unlike, neither is it made like nor unlike. And

b in going from small to great and to equal and vice-versa, it's neither small nor great nor equal, neither would it be increasing nor diminishing nor being made equal.

It doesn't look like it.

So the One would suffer all these experiences, if it *is*.

How not?

What, properly, would the different things experience if one *is* — mustn't this be looked into?[16]

It must be looked into.

Shall we say, then, if one *is*, what the things different from the One must have experienced?

Let's say it.

Now if in fact they are different than the One, the different things are not the One. For otherwise they would not be different than the One.

157c   Right.

However, neither are the different things entirely devoid of the One; instead, they partake of it in a way.

In what way?

Because surely the things different than the One are different since they have pieces. For if they should have no pieces, they would be completely one.

Right.

But pieces, we say, belong to whatever is a whole.

Yes, we say this.

And yet the very whole must be, by necessity, one thing made up of many things — this whole of which the pieces will be pieces. For each of the pieces must be a piece not of many but of a whole.

How's that?

If something should be a piece of many things, among which it's
d a member, surely it will be a piece of itself, which is impossible, and it will be a piece of each one of the different things, then, if in fact of all. For should it not be a piece of one, it will belong to the rest except this one, and so it will not be a piece of each one, and by not being a piece of each it will belong to none of the many. But should it belong to

---

[16] Parmenides now begins the third argument. His hypothesis is still that "one is," but now he describes the results for all the things different than the One, the "different things." The argument runs from 157b6 to 159b1.

none, it's impossible for it to belong — as a piece or as anything else — to all these things, of which it belongs to none at all.

That's certainly apparent.

The piece, then, is not a piece of the many nor of all things, but of
157e one certain idea, a certain one which we call 'whole': out of all things, it's the one that has come into being completely. Of this, the piece would be a piece.

Entirely so.

If, then, the different things have pieces, they would partake of both the Whole and one.

Of course.

Then the things different than the One necessarily are one complete whole that has pieces.

Necessarily.

And, in fact, the same explanation also holds for each piece: it
158a must, by necessity, partake of the One. For if each of them is a piece, then surely the 'each' signifies that it's one, when delineated from the rest, in itself — if in fact it will be 'each.'

Right.

But, to be sure, should it partake of the One, it'd make clear that it is different than one. For otherwise it wouldn't partake, but rather it would be one. But now it's clearly impossible for anything except the One itself to be one.

Impossible.

But it's necessary for both the Whole and the Piece to partake of the One. For the former will be one whole, of which the pieces are pieces; but each of the latter will be one piece of the Whole, in turn — as long as it's a piece of a whole.

That's so.

b   And so the things partaking of the One will partake while being other than it?

How not?

But the things other than the One would surely be many. For if the things different than the One were neither one nor more than one, they would be nothing.

No, they wouldn't.

But since whatever partakes of the One as a piece and of the One as a whole is more than one, isn't it now necessary for these things to be limitless in multitude, these very things which come to partake of the One?

How?

Let's see this way: does 'to come to partake' mean anything else than that they are not one nor do they partake of the One at that time when they are coming to partake?

That's clear.

158c   And so they are multitudes in which the One isn't present?

Sure, multitudes.

What then? If we should be able to abstract, with our understanding, from such things the very least thing we could, isn't it necessary for this abstracted thing, since it would not partake of the One, also to be a multitude and not one?

Necessarily.

And so whenever we look into this other nature, in itself, of the form, however much of it as we can see at any one time, it will always be boundless in multitude?

Entirely so.

d   And yet whenever each one piece becomes a piece, they already possess a limit in relation to one another and in relation to the whole, and the whole in relation to the parts.

Exactly so.

For the things different than the One, then, the result is that, from the One and from their being in community, so it looks, something other comes into being in themselves, something that provides a limit for them in relation to one another. But their nature, as far as they are concerned, is limitless.

It appears.

So clearly the things different than the One are limitless both as wholes and as concerns their parts and also partake of a limit.

Of course.

e   And so they are both like and unlike both one another and themselves?

In what way?

Surely insofar as they are all limitless in respect to their own nature, this way they would have experienced the same thing.

Of course.

And, in addition, insofar as they all partake of a limit — this way, as well, they all would have experienced the same thing.

How not?

But insofar as they have experienced being both limited and limitless, they have suffered these experiences which are experiences most opposed to one another.

159a   Yes.

But opposites are surely as unlike as possible.

Why, how not?

In the case of each single experience, then, they would be like both themselves and each other; but in the case of both experiences together they are both most opposed and unlike.

I'm afraid so.

So clearly the different things themselves would be both like and unlike both themselves and each other.

That's so.

And they're the same as and other than one another, and are in motion and stand at rest — and with no difficulty we will find that the things different than the One suffer all those opposite experiences, since,
b   in fact, they obviously have experienced these ones.

You're right.

And so, if we dismiss these things as already apparent, let us inquire once again if one *is*, are the things different from the One only this way or not?[17]

Of course.

So let's say from the beginning if one *is*, what the things different from the One must have experienced.

Yes, let's say it.

Isn't the One separate from the different things, and the different

---

[17] This argument, the fourth, extends from 159b2 to 160b1. Like the third, the hypothesis is that "one is," and the results are shown for the "different things." But all the results of this argument contradict those of the third. The relation of the two is similar to that of the first and second arguments. The reader should note that, of the first four arguments, the fourth is the shortest, just as the eight is the shortest of the last four.

things from the One?

Why's that?

Because surely there's nothing other besides them — something different than the One yet different than the different things. For every-
159c thing is spoken of when one says, 'Both the One and the different things.'

Yes, everything.

Then there's nothing other than these, in which the One and the different things could *be*, as if in the same thing.

No, there isn't.

So the One and the different things are never in the same thing.

It doesn't look like it.

They're separate then?

Yes.

Nor do we say that the One, in the true sense, has pieces.

How could it?

d   The One, then, would not be in the different things as a whole nor would pieces of it, if it both is separate from the different things and has no pieces.

How could it?

In no way, then, would the different things partake of the One, since they partake of it neither by any piece nor as a whole.

It doesn't look like it.

In no way, then, are the different things one, nor do they have any one in themselves.

No, they don't.

So neither are the different things many: for each one of them would be a piece of the whole, if they were many. But now the things different than the One are neither one nor many nor whole nor pieces, since in no way do they partake of it.

Right.

Then the different things themselves are not two or three nor are these things present in them, if in fact they are in every way devoid of
e   the One.

That's so.

And, then, the different things themselves are not like and are not unlike the One, nor is Likeness and Unlikeness present in them. For if they should be like and unlike or should possess Likeness and Unlikeness in themselves, surely the things different than the One would possess in themselves two forms opposed to one another.

It appears.

But it would be impossible, at any rate, for whatever does not partake of one to partake of any two.

Impossible.

The different things, then, are neither like nor unlike nor both. 160a For should they be like or unlike, they would partake of one or the other form; and should they be both, they would partake of two opposed forms. And this is obviously impossible.

True.

Then they're also not the same or other, nor in motion or standing at rest, nor becoming or perishing, nor greater or less or equal, nor have they experienced anything else of such things. For if the different things submit to having experienced any such thing, they will partake of one and two and three and odd and even — things it's obviously b impossible for them to partake of, since they're devoid of the One in every way whatsoever.

Most true.

So, clearly, if one *is*, the one both is all things and is not even one thing both in relation to itself and likewise in relation to the different things.[18]

Completely so.

So be it. After this mustn't we look into what must result if, in fact, the One *is* not?[19]

Yes, we must look into it.

---

[18] In this one line Parmenides succinctly states the results of the preceding four arguments. Arguments one and three show that, if one is, it is nothing. (Argument three makes this point indirectly. If the things different than the One experience everything, then, to be different than them, mustn't the One experience nothing?) Arguments two and four, likewise, show that, if One is, it is everything. The major theme is constant, "one is," but the variations on that theme result in complete contradiction. Compare his summary here to the one that follows the final 'movement' of the piece (166c2-6).

[19] Parmenides now changes the basic hypothesis from "one is" to "the One is not." With this change he begins the fifth argument, which runs from 160b5 to 163b6. In this argument he deduces the results of this hypothesis for the One itself.

What sort of thing, then, would this hypothesis — 'if one *is* not' — be? Does it differ at all from this one: 'if not-one *is* not?'

Sure it differs.

160c   Does it only differ, or is to say 'if not-one *is* not' the total opposite of 'if one *is* not?'

The total opposite.

But what if someone should say 'if Greatness *is* not' or 'Smallness *is* not' or anything else of that sort, then wouldn't he in each case make clear that he means that whatever *is* not is something other?

Of course.

And so also now he would make clear that he means that whatever *is* not is other than the different things, whenever he says, 'if one *is* not.' And do we understand what he means?

We understand.

Therefore he first means something known and then something other than the different things, whenever he says 'one,' whether he

d   adds *being* or *not-being* to it. For whatever is said not to *be* is nonetheless known, and it is known to differ from the different things. Or not?

Necessarily.

In this way, then, we must say from the beginning, if one *is* not, what must be. First of all this must, so it looks, be the case concerning it: there is knowledge of it. Otherwise there'd be no way to know what is said whenever someone says, 'If one *is* not.'

True.

And so mustn't the different things also be other than it, or else it wouldn't be said to be other than the different things?

Of course.

And so otherness, in addition to knowledge, belongs to it. For

e   whenever someone says that the One is other than the different things, he doesn't mean that otherness belongs to the different things, but rather to it.

It appears.

In addition the One that is not partakes of the 'of that' and the 'of something' and the 'of this' and the 'to this' and the 'of these' and of all such things. For the One could not be spoken of nor could anything be said to be other than the One, nor could anything be or be said to be to it or of it, unless it had a share in the 'of something' or of these different things.

Right.

So it's not possible for the One to *be*, since it really *is* not, but in no way is it prohibited from partaking of many things; in fact, it's nec-
161a essary for it to do this, if indeed that One and not something different *is* not. However, if neither the One nor the 'that' will not *be*, then the speech is about something different and nothing can be uttered. But if that One and nothing else is hypothesized not to *be*, then it's necessary for it to have a share in the 'that' and many different things.

Yes, of course.

Then it also possesses Unlikeness in relation to the different things. For should the things different than the One be other, they would be of another sort.

Yes.

But aren't things of another sort of a different sort?

How not?

But aren't things of a different sort unlike?

b   Yes, unlike.

And so if in fact they are unlike the One, it's clear that the unlike things would be unlike something unlike them.

Clearly.

So the One would possess Unlikeness, in respect to which the different things are unlike it.

It looks that way.

But if being unlike the different things belongs to it, isn't it necessary that being like itself belong to it?

How?

If being unlike one belongs to the One, surely the speech would not concern something like the One, nor would the hypothesis be about the One, but rather about something different than one.

Of course.

c   But certainly this can't be.

Certainly not.

Therefore being like the One, itself, must belong to it.

It must.

And, in addition, it is not, in turn, equal to the different things. For if it should be equal, it would already *be* and be like them by this equality. And both of these things are impossible, if indeed one *is* not.

Yes, impossible.

And since it is not equal to the different things, isn't it also necessary for the different things not to be equal to it?

Necessarily.

But aren't things not equal unequal?

Yes.

But aren't unequals unequal to something unequal to them?

How not?

And so the One partakes of Inequality, in respect to which the
160d different things are unequal to it?

It does partake.

But surely both Greatness and Smallness belong to Inequality.

Yes, they do.

There's both Greatness and Smallness, then, in a one of this sort?

I'm afraid so.

Surely Greatness and Smallness are always most removed from one another.

Of course.

Then there's always something between them.

There is.

Can you say, then, anything else that's between them except Equality?

No, only this.

Whatever, then, possesses Greatness and Smallness, also possesses Equality, since it's between these two.

e   It appears.

The One that is not, so it looks, would have a share of Equality and Greatness and Smallness.

It looks that way.

And yet it must also, in a way, partake of beinghood.

How's that?

It must *be* in the state that we've been speaking of: for if it's not in this state, we would not be speaking truly when we say that the One *is* not. But if we are speaking truly, it is clear that we are saying the very things that *are*. Or is it not so?

Yes, that's so.

But since we claim to speak truly, it's necessary for us also to claim
162a to speak the things that *are*.

Necessarily.

So it looks, then, as though the One that *is* not, *is*. For if it's not
to be something that *is* not, and instead will somehow let go of *being* in
order to give way to *not-being*, straight away it will be something that
is.

Entirely so.

It must, therefore, possess, as a restraint on its *not-being*, *being*
something that *is* not, — if it's going not to *be*. In the same way Being
must possess Non-being as its *not-being*, so that it may, in turn, *be* completely. For in this way Being would most of all *be* and Non-being would
most of all not *be*. For Being will partake of the beinghood of *being*
something that *is*, but will not partake of the beinghood of *being* some-
b thing that *is* not, if it's going to *be* completely. And Non-being will not
partake of the beinghood of *not-being* something that *is* not, but will
partake of the beinghood of *being* something that *is* not, if Non-being,
in turn, also will completely not *be*.

Most true!

And so, since in fact Being has a share in *not-being* and Non-
being in *being*, then the One, since it *is* not, must, by necessity, have a
share in *being* in order not to *be*.

Necessarily.

And so the One appears to possess beinghood, if it *is* not.

It appears.

Also, then, no beinghood, since, in fact, it *is* not.

How not?

Well, is something that's a certain way able not to be that way,
while not changing from that state?

No, it's not able to.

c   So whenever something both is and then is not a certain way, it
always signifies a change.

How not?

But change is a motion. Or what will we say?

A motion.

Now, the One obviously both *is* and *is* not?

Yes.

Then obviously it is one way and then not this way.

It looks like it.

And the non-being which is one, therefore, has been shown to move, since it has a change from *being* to *not-being*.

I'm afraid so.

And yet if it's nowhere among the beings — as, in fact, it isn't, since it *is* not —, then it would not withdraw from somewhere to somewhere else.

How would it?

162d   It wouldn't move, then, by changing place, at any rate.

No, it wouldn't.

Nor, indeed, would it turn about in the same thing: for it nowhere touches upon the same thing. For 'the same thing' is something that *is*, and it's impossible for what *is* not to be in one of the things that *are*.

Yes, impossible.

The One that *is* not, then, couldn't turn about in some place that it's not in.

No, it couldn't.

Nor, indeed, can the One change from itself, whether it *is* or *is* not. For then the speech would not still be about the One — if in fact it changed from itself — but rather about something different.

Right.

But if it neither changes nor turns about in the same place nor changes place, would it somehow still be in motion?

e   How could it?

But whatever's motionless necessarily is at peace, and whatever's at peace necessarily stands at rest.

Necessarily.

The One that in no way *is*, then, so it looks, both stands at rest and is in motion.

It looks that way.

And yet if indeed it is in motion, a great necessity forces it to
163a change. For in whatever way it be moved, in this respect it no longer is as it was, but is otherwise.

That's so.

So by moving the One also changes.

Yes.

And yet by not moving in any way it in no way changes.

No, it doesn't.

Insofar, then, as the non-being that's one is in motion, it changes; but insofar as it's not in motion, it doesn't change.

No, it doesn't.

The One that is not, then, both changes and does not change.

It appears.

But isn't it necessary for whatever changes to become other than 163b it was before, and to perish from its previous state? But what does not change mustn't come to be nor perish?

Necessarily.

And the One that is not, then, by changing, both comes to be and perishes; but, by not changing, it neither comes to be nor perishes. And so the One that is not both comes to be and perishes and neither comes to be nor perishes.

No, it certainly doesn't.

Once more let's go back again to the beginning to see whether these things appear to us as they do now, or otherwise.

Well, we must.

c   And so if one *is* not, we'll say what the result concerning it must be?[20]

Yes.

But whenever we say '*is* not,' does it signify anything else than a deprivation of beinghood for whatever we say *is* not?

Nothing else.

Then whenever we say something *is* not, do we mean that it *is* not one way but *is* another? Or does this '*is* not,' once uttered, simply sig-

---

[20] This is the beginning of the sixth argument, which, like the fifth, treats of the hypothesis "one *is* not." Similarly, like the fifth, second and first arguments, the sixth deduces the results of this hypothesis for the One itself. It goes from 163b7 to 164b4. As you may expect, from your experience of arguments two and four, this argument contradicts the preceeding one in its entirety.

nify that whatever *is* not — no way, no how — *is*, nor in any way partakes of beinghood?

Most simply — that's it.

Then whatever *is* not could neither *be* nor partake of beinghood in any different way.

163d No, it couldn't.

But would becoming and perishing be anything else than, for the former, to come to partake of beinghood, or, for the latter, to lose beinghood?

Nothing else.

But whatever has no share in something would neither take hold of it nor lose it.

How could it?

The One, then, since it in no way *is*, must not possess nor give up nor come to partake in beinghood in any way.

That's likely.

So the non-being that's one neither perishes nor comes to be, since in no way does it partake of beinghood.

It appears not.

e Nor, then, does it change at all: for it would then both come to be and perish, should it suffer this.

True.

But if it doesn't change, isn't it necessary that it not be in motion?

Necessarily.

Nor, indeed, will we say that what in no way *is* stands at rest. For whatever stands at rest must always be in the same place.

The same, how not?

So, in turn, whatever *is* not, we shall say, never stands at rest nor is in motion.

No, not at all.

164a In addition, it does not possess any of the beings; for whenever it partakes of a certain being, it would partake of beinghood.

Clearly.

Nor, then, does it possess Greatness nor Smallness nor Equality.

No, it doesn't.

Nor, indeed, would it possess Likeness or Otherness either in relation to itself or in relation to the different things.

It appears not.

But what? How could the different things relate to it, if nothing must relate to it?

They cannot.

The different things, then, are neither like nor unlike nor the same as nor other than it.

No, they aren't.

But what? Will there be the 'of that' or the 'to that' or the 'something' or the 'this' or the 'of this' or 'of a different thing' or 'to a different thing' or 'once' or 'hereafter' or 'now' or knowledge or opinion or perception or definition or name or anything else of the things that *are* concerning the thing that *is* not?

164b

No, there won't.

So, then, one that *is* not somehow is in no state at all.

It certainly looks as though it is in no state at all.

So let's say once again, if one *is* not, what the different things must have experienced.[21]

Yes, let's say it.

Well surely they must *be*: for if the different things were not, nothing could be said about the different things.

That's so.

But if this speech is about the different things, these different things are other. Or don't you assign the 'different' and the 'other' to the same thing?

c

I do.

But doubtless we claim that the other is other than another and the different is different than something different?

Yes.

And for the different things, then, if they're going to be different, there is something they are different from.

Necessarily.

But what could it be? For they won't be different than the One, since it *is* not.

---

[21] We now begin the seventh argument. The hypothesis is still that "one *is* not," but here we deduce the results for the "different things." The argument extends from 164b5 to 165e1.

No, they won't.

They're different than one another, then. For this is all that's left to them, or else they're different than nothing.

Right.

Then they're all different from one another in multitude; for they could not be so one by one, since one *is* not. Instead each heap of **164d** them, so it looks, is limitless in multitude. For even if someone shall grasp what seems to be the smallest thing, just like a dream in sleep there appears instantaneously a many in the place of what seemed to be one, and in the place of the smallest thing there appears something very great in relation to anything chopped off from it.

Absolutely right.

So, if there be heaps of this sort, the different things would be different than one another — if one *is* not but different things *are*.

Exactly so.

And so will there be many heaps, each appearing to be one but not really being so, if in fact there'll *be* no one?

That's so.

And number will seem to belong to them, if in fact each seems to **e** be one while they are many.

Of course.

And so some will appear to be odd and others even — but they won't be so in truth, if in fact there'll *be* no one.

No, they won't be so.

In addition, we claim, there will seem to be a smallest thing present among them; but this appears many and great in relation to each of the **165a** many apparently small things that there are.

How not?

And, to be sure, each heap will be thought to be equal to the many small things. For it would pass from greater to less, it appears, before seeming to enter into the middle — but this would be an appearance of equality.

That's likely.

And so, while having a limit in relation to a different heap, does it have in relation to itself neither beginning nor limit nor middle?

Why's that?

Because whenever someone, by his understanding, takes hold of one of these things as belonging to such heaps, then a different begin-

165b ning will always appear before the beginning, and another end will be left over after the end, and in the middle there'll be different middles more middle than the middle — but smaller, since we can't grasp each one of them because the One *is* not.

Most true.

So I believe that anything that is, whatever someone grasps with his understanding, necessarily is smashed into chopped-up bits. For surely, without one, he would always grasp a heap.

Of course.

c   And so to anyone seeing such a thing from afar and faintly, won't it necessarily appear to be one? But to someone thinking about it up close and sharply, doesn't each one appear limitless in multitude, if in fact it's devoid of the One that *is* not?

Yes, that's most necessary.

So, then, each of the different things must appear to be both limitless and having limit and one and many, if one *is* not but the things different from the One *are*.

They must.

And so will they also seem to be both like and unlike?

How's that?

Just as to someone standing far from a drawing, everything there, appearing to be one, appears to have experienced the same situation and to be alike —

Of course.

d   — But when he comes closer they appear many and other and, by the appearance of the Other, of another sort and unlike themselves.

That's so.

And so it's necessary for these very heaps to appear both like and unlike themselves and one another.

Of course.

And so also the same and other as one another, and touching and separate from themselves, and moving in every motion and standing altogether at rest, and becoming and perishing and neither, and surely every sort of thing that we can easily describe, if, without there being

e one, many *is*.

Yes, most true.

Going back once more to the beginning, let's say, if one *is* not, but the things different than the One *are*, what must be.[22]

Let's say it then.

Now the different things won't be one.

How could they?

Nor, then, many: for one would also be present in beings that are many. For if one is not in these things at all, then they're all no-thing, so that they would not even be many.

True.

But should one not be present in the different things, the different things are neither many nor one.

No, they aren't.

166a   Nor do they appear one or many.

Why's that?

Because the different things have no community — no way, no how — with any of the things that *are* not; nor do any of the things that *are* not relate to any of the different things. For the things that *are* not have no part.

True.

Then there would be no opinion about anything that *is* not among the different things, nor any appearance, and — no way, no how — whatever *is* not is not opined by the different things.

No, it isn't.

If one, then, *is* not, none of the different things are opined to be **b** one or many: for without one it's impossible to opine 'many.'

Yes, impossible.

If one, then, *is* not, the different things neither are nor are opined to be one or many.

It doesn't look like it.

Then not like or unlike.

No.

---

[22] This argument, number eight, is the shortest of them all, running only from 165e2 to 166c2. Like number seven, it assumes that "one is not," and it deduces the results for the different things, but it comes to a completely opposed conclusion. With this final point and counter-point of contradiction, Parmenides' song is complete.

And not, surely, the same or other, nor touching nor separate, nor anything else that before we described them as appearing to be. The different things neither are nor appear to be any of these, if one *is* not.

True.

166c   And so, if we should say in short, "If one *is* not, nothing *is*," would we speak rightly?

Entirely so.

Let this be said, then, and also that, so it looks, whether one *is* or *is* not, both it and the different things, both in relation to themselves and in relation to each other, all, in all ways, both *are* and *are* not and both appear and do not appear.[23]

Most true.

---

[23] Compare this summary, one that encompasses all eight arguments, with the one that capped the fourth argument (160b2-5). In this final summation the gracious Parmenides gives equal prominence to the "different things," that is, the negation of the One. Likewise, he put appearance on par with being. This majestic finalé thus encompasses the whole, "all, in all ways."

Glossary and Index of Major Terms

If you have read through the entire dialogue, you know that the major terms of the discussion are entirely wound around one another and interconnected. While speaking of like and unlike Parmenides may bring in same and other. Or when demonstrating that the One or the different things suffer any sort of changes, he may pin his argument on an understanding of motion and rest. To index every appearance of every major term would be to dissolve this complex structure into an atomic soup. I doubt that such dissolution would help the student. Likewise, as I argued in the Introduction, a major theme of this work is to make us marvel that the most simple ideas defy exact representation in our speech (and hence our writing). Since Parmenides' arguments teach us to eschew the calcification of these terms, a traditional glossary would be counter-productive.

Nevertheless, to highlight the dialogue's major treatments of these major terms is a good way to further Parmenides' project. Such a general index allows the student, once the dialogue has been read, to shuttle back and forth more easily between Parmenides' discussions of these terms. One can thereby see more clearly the different and perhaps conflicting senses of words such as being, not-being, limit and limitlessness. Whatever glosses, then, with which I may precede an entry, are not meant to "explain" the term or terms in all of their appearances in the dialogue. Rather, I offer but a few, simple etymological insights into the words, ones well known to students of Greek.

I have ordered the following terms as they appear in the dialogue. Any Roman numerals refer to the arguments, as I numbered them in the "Outline" in the Introduction. (I.e., II is argument two, VI is argument six, etc.)

One and Many

One should be careful to distinguish "one" or "the One" from our word "unit" (which in Greek would be μονὰς); likewise keep "many" separate from "multitude" (Greek πλῆθος).

Major discussions: 127e-129e, 136a, I-VIII.137b-166c, II.143c-144e, 156b, 157a, VIII.165e-166b.

Like and Unlike

The following list includes discussions of the forms of Likeness and Unlikeness.

Major discussions: 127e-129e, 130b, 130e, 132d-133a, 136b, I.139e-140b, II.147c-148d, 156b, 157a, III.158e-159a, IV.159e-160a, V.161a-c, VI.164a, VIII.166b.

Rest and Motion

The Greek word for "rest," στάσις, comes from the verb "to stand." Thus my translation "standing at rest." The word for "motion," κίνησις, implies not only physical locomotion but also all types of change.

Major discussions: 129e, 136b, I.138b-139b, II.145e-146a, 156c-157a, III.159a, IV.160a, V.162b-163a, VI.163e, VII.165d.

Great, Small and Equal

These are the terms used in weighing, fathoming, calculating or otherwise measuring any sort of magnitude or multitude. In the dialogue, Parmenides treats them as questionable in themselves; in the sciences of arithmetic or geometry, they are treated as understood terms, which are then predicated of other things.

Major discussions: 131a, 131d-132a, I.140b-d, II.149d-151e, 156b, 157b, IV.160a, V.160c, V.161c-e, VI.164a, VII.164e-165b.

Becoming, Perishing and Age

As I mention in the Translator's Note, "to come into being" is the translation of the Greek γίγνεσθαι, which can also mean "to be born." From this verb we get the English "genesis" and "generation." Sometimes opposed to this concept is "corruption" (from the verb "to corrupt," which can also have moral connotations) and othertimes "perishing." The Greek for "age" has nothing to do linguistically with coming to be or passing away.

Major discussions: 136b, I.140e-141d, II.151e-155e, 156a-b, 157a, IV.160a, V.163b, VI.163d-e, VII.165d.

Being and Non-being

See the Translator's Note for the various words connected to the verb "to be" and their translations.

Major discussions: 136b, I.141d-142a, II.142b-143b, 155e-156a, 157a, V.160b-161c, V.161e-162b, VI.163b-d.

Part and Whole

The Greek for "part" is μόρος and "piece" is μόριον. They are close but not identical. "Whole" is ὅλον, which, with the article, can mean "the Whole" of things in the sense of the Universe.

Major discussions: I.137c-d, II.142c-143a, III.157b-158b, IV.159b-e.

Limit, Limitlessness and Shape

Another translation for "limit" could be boundary or end and for "limitless," infinite (literally, "without an end").

Major discussions: I.137d-138a, II.144e-145a, III.158b-d, VII.164d, VII.165c-d.

Location

There is no exact Greek word which I translate as "location." Rather, the following citations refer to discussions of the One or the different things being "in" themselves or "in" something else. I also include places where Parmenides describes them as "touching" themselves or one another, as the idea of touching demands a sense of location.

Major discussions: I.138a-b, II.145b-e, II.148d-149d, IV.159a, VII.165d, VIII.166b.

Same and Other

Greek uses the intensive pronoun to mean "same." Thus, in Greek, the phrase "the same man" differs from "the man himself" only by word order. In my translation, "other" differs from "different" (as in "the different things") in the same way as Latin *alter* differs from *alius*. In English, alter means "the other of two," while *alius* is "another" (out of many others, perhaps).

Major discussions: I.139c-e, II.146a-147b, III.159a, IV.160a, VI.164a, VII.164b-c, VII.165d.